The Protea Book

ᴇGEˢ

The Protea Book

A GUIDE TO CULTIVATED PROTEACEAE

Lewis J. Matthews

TIMBER PRESS
Portland, Oregon

First published in North America
and the United Kingdom in 2002 by
Timber Press, Inc.
The Haseltine Building
133 S.W. Second Avenue, Suite 450
Portland, Oregon 97204, USA

orders@timberpress.com
www.timberpress.com

ISBN 0-88192-553-5

A catalog record for this book is available from
the Library of Congress

Designed and typeset by Richard King
at Canterbury University Press

Printed by Rainbow Print, Christchurch, New Zealand

Cover: *Protea cynaroides*
Frontispiece: *Banksia speciosa*

This book is dedicated to my late parents, Barbara and Jim (J. W.) Matthews,
devoted plantspeople and career journalists who not only encouraged me
to become involved with both horticulture and writing, with the many facets
involved in these passions, but also gave me lifetime inspiration through
their own books, magazines and other journalistic endeavours.

Contents

Acknowledgements

For more than 30 years a great many people with a love of plants and gardens have provided me with inspiration, information, access to their gardens for photographic purposes and generally aided me with the writing and publication of my books.

Ian and Jocelyn Bell, Wanganui, New Zealand, for information.

Dr Peter Harper, University of Canterbury, New Zealand, for his expert advice and tuition in his photography courses.

Jack Hobbs, Curator/Manager, Auckland Regional Botanic Gardens, New Zealand, for information and use of photographs.

Geoff Jewell, Te Horo Ornamentals, New Zealand, for information, access to his nursery and plants and supplying flowers to photograph.

Richard King, editor at Canterbury University Press, for his professionalism, design skills and encouragement during the production of this book.

Dr William G. Lee, Landcare Research, Dunedin, New Zealand, for introductory paragraph to *Knightia*, referring to prehistoric Proteaceae in New Zealand.

Andrew and David Mathews, Proteaflora Nursery, Victoria, Australia, for use of some photographs, information and access to their plants and nursery.

Kaye Matthews, my wife, for her wide-ranging help and encouragement over the years.

Ray Noonan, Christchurch, New Zealand, for allowing unlimited access to his extensive collection of proteaceae for photography purposes.

Dr Phil Parvin, formerly of the University of Hawaii, for information.

Dr John Rourke, the Compton Herbarium, Cape Town, South Africa, for encouragement and information.

There have been numerous other enthusiasts (too many to list here) who have allowed me free access to their gardens over the years . Please accept this acknowledgement and my grateful thanks.

Lewis Matthews

Photography

The majority of photographs used in this book were taken by the author using Nikon photographic equipment and Fujichrome Velvia and Provia colour slide film.

Other people supplying photographs are acknowledged below with gratitude:

George Fuller, New Plymouth, New Zealand (*Protea rubropilosa*)

Jack Hobbs, Curator/Manager Auckland Regional Botanic Gardens, New Zealand (*Alloxylon pinnatum, Leucadendron* 'Amy', *Toronia toru*)

Geoff Jewell, Te Horo Ornamentals, New Zealand (*Telopea speciosissima* 'Wirrimbirra White')

Dr Stephan Halloy, Scientist, New Zealand Institute for Crop & Food Research Limited, Invermay, New Zealand (*Gevuina avellana* flowers and fruit)

Andrew and David Mathews, Proteaflora Nursery, Victoria, Australia (*Banksia ashbyii, B. burdettii,* and *B.* 'Waite Orange')

Iain Gillespie, *Sydney Morning Herald*, Sydney, Australia (Cathy Freeman being presented with gold medal and bouquet of Australian wildflowers at the 2001 Sydney Olympics)

RIGHT: *Protea holosericea.*

Introduction

WHAT IS A 'PROTEA'?

Most members of the family Proteaceae have become referred to simply as 'proteas', and this naming even has the approval of the International Protea Association. In line with this approach to terminology, *The Protea Book* covers the family rather than just the genus *Protea*; strictly it should have been titled *The Proteaceae Book*. The purists, especially in South Africa, are understandably concerned at this application of the term 'protea' and are now tending to refer to the South African *Protea* genus collectively by its old common name, sugarbushes.

Just a decade or so ago gardeners would speak of leucospermum or leucadendron species or cultivars, but now the tendency is to refer to them all as simply 'proteas'. Likewise with the banksias, telopeas, grevilleas, serrurias and a number of the other genera.

It was Carl Linnaeus, the famous Swedish botanist, who in 1735 classified the proteas. Observing the variations in 24 historic engravings of what we now know as *Leucadendron*, *Leucospermum*, *Mimetes* and *Protea*, he named them all after the legendary Greek sea god Proteus, who could change his shape at will. He was, of course, referring to the surprising diversity of flower and foliage depicted. In 1809 Robert Brown revised the classification of the family and described some 39 species of the actual *Protea* genus as well as others.

There are currently some 73 genera and more than 1,500 species in the family Proteaceae, and from time to time a new species is discovered. The greatest number – some 800 species – originate from Australia, while around 400 occur in Africa (330 in the south-western Cape alone). Approximately 90 species are found in Central and South America, while the rest are scattered through Madagascar, New Guinea, New Caledonia, South-east Asia and New Zealand.

Adding to the intrigue of this plant family is the ever-increasing number of cultivars being developed.

LEFT: *Leucadendron* 'Safari Sunset' at the late-winter 'rainbow' stage.

From as early as the eighteenth century proteas intrigued botanical artists, and numerous historic engravings are preserved that capture both the beauty of the flowers and the enthusiasm of the artists. This example of *Protea cordata* was published in *Curtis's Botanical Magazine* in 1803.

Manipulated hybrids often have significant advantages over the species, whether to satisfy the demanding cut-flower markets with better colours, longer stems and increased vase life, or for the vigour, ease of cultivation and disease resistance that the home gardener desires.

ORIGINS

The forerunner of today's proteas existed some 80 million years ago. As the supercontinent Gondwana

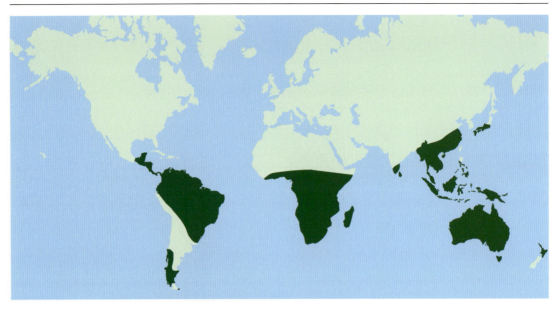

Natural distribution of the family Proteaceae.

separated into drifting landmasses that became Antarctica, Africa, India, Australia, New Zealand, New Guinea and many of the Pacific Islands, it is believed that the family Proteaceae was widely dispersed, then evolved to produce many amazingly diverse and geographically scattered genera.

When it is realised that different species of *Lomatia* are found in both Australia and South America; that one of the northern Australian *Banksia* species (*B. denudata*) is also found growing naturally in Papua New Guinea and some islands; that *Oreocallis* species occur in Australia, New Guinea and South America, and some *Macadamia* species are found in New Caledonia as well as Australia, one can easily see the rationale behind the scientific papers that have presented the theories.

THE FASCINATION OF PROTEAS

It is usually the exotic appearance of protea flower heads that first grabs the attention of the average florist's window shopper or gardener seeking to cultivate these dramatic plants. Their fascinating charms range from the massive king protea, through the vivid orange or yellow leucospermums (or 'pins' as they are called in Hawaii) and brilliant red club-shaped waratahs, to the colourful leaf bracts of leucadendrons, the exquisitely dainty pink-and-white *Serruria florida* (blushing bride) and the curious cones of the Australian banksias.

Proteas are increasingly being used by florists and

floral designers to make powerful 'architectural' statements. Bold arrangements are frequently seen in the foyers of corporate headquarters, in homes and offices, and in television show décor. Their typically strong colours and striking appearance make proteas an ideal choice of flower for arrangements in modern, minimalist buildings. At the 2000 Olympic Games in Sydney, bouquets presented to medal winners comprised mixtures of Australian native flora, and pre-eminent among these were waratahs and banksias. So proteas shared the world stage with the athletes.

Beyond the initial reaction to the uniquely spectacular flowers, the next thing to register is just how different are the various members of the family. It is almost incomprehensible to a layperson that the spidery flowers of a grevillea, the massive cones of a banksia, the dinner-plate-size flowers of a king protea, the dainty nodding *Protea nana*, and the macadamia nut are all proteas. Even the foliage varies greatly, from quite narrow and almost needle-like (*Protea aristata*) to large, broad and leathery (*Protea cynaroides*), through thick and serrated (*Banksia* spp.) to soft and covered with silky hairs (*Leucadendron argenteum*).

Another advantage for both the home flower arranger and the commercial florist is that proteas offer exceptional vase life. Given the usual care that cut flowers need for longevity – changing water regularly, re-cutting ends of stems and using some preservative in the water – these flowers will give weeks of pleasure. In fact, many will eventually dry off in their vases and become semi-permanent arrangements.

The home gardener who plants proteas must forego many habits that may have been instilled over the years. Proteas practically 'thrive on neglect' and can be 'killed with kindness'.

Excessive watering must be avoided, as proteas do not tolerate wet soil conditions. Good drainage, almost without exception, is the first rule for successful cultivation, and proteas generally thrive in open, sunny positions. Because most originate from quite harsh environments where nutrient levels are low, proteas have developed a root system that enables them to cope accordingly. As a result, except in poor soils, fertilisers are to be avoided, especially those that contain phosphate, which is toxic to the Proteaceae.

RIGHT: Australian athlete Cathy Freeman after winning the gold medal for the 400 metres, as with all medal winners at the Sydney 2000 Olympic Games, was presented with a spectacular floral bouquet of Australian wildflowers with New South Wales waratah (*Telopea speciosissima*) particularly prominent.

BELOW: This popular stamp issue in South Africa during the 1960s and 1970s depicted a comprehensive range of that country's indigenous Proteaceae species. Significantly, the South African national cricket and netball teams are known as the Proteas.

Cultivating proteas

Most of the best-known Proteaceae genera and species in both South Africa and Australia have adapted to relatively harsh environments that are often surprisingly arid and low in nutrients. In some soils the pH may be as low as 3, extremely acidic, where nutrients are difficult for plants to access. To cope with these difficulties the plants evolved a 'proteoid root system', the understanding of which is the key to successful protea cultivation.

Proteoid rootlets are tufts of fine white waxy rootlets extending from the main roots. They seem to be more prevalent during the more active growing periods of spring and autumn, and are often close to the surface of the soil. These roots are specialised to extract nutrients from poor soils, so applying fertilisers is obviously going to affect them. Basically, the rootlets either do not develop or are killed off because of excess nutrients, especially phosphorus. This may not become apparent immediately, but once the plant is stressed by dry weather or heavy flowering, the lack of proteoid rootlets means the plant cannot obtain enough water, which will inevitably result in its collapse. Similarly, excessive water can prevent aeration of the soil around the root area (the waterlogging typical of heavy, non-porous soils) and lead to rotting of the roots. However, most proteas actually thrive on quite large amounts of water provided the soil is well drained. In fact, plentiful water is believed to help wash away the salts that accumulate to toxic levels in a drought. Most knowledgeable botanists and horticulturists consider it a fallacy to call proteas 'drought-resistant': good drainage plus ample water is essential in the successful cultivation of these plants.

Because the proteoid root system is found mainly near the surface of the soil, among leaf litter, other organic material and associated fungal hyphae, hoeing or other cultivation techniques can be detrimental and should be avoided. This surface layer of organic matter appears essential to the health of the roots but can be substituted to some extent in a home-garden situation by a lawn around the plants, provided that lawn fertiliser is avoided in their proximity.

REQUIREMENTS

Soil types and drainage

Proteas will thrive in stony, gravelly, sandy soil, as well as good silts or loam, provided it is free-draining. Even heavy river silt can grow proteas successfully if it overlies gravel. Drainage can be improved by raising planting beds. Raised planters or plots may have a layer of gravel or rubble placed on the existing soil before backfilling with soil to further facilitate drainage.

Some species are more tolerant of poor drainage provided they are not constantly wet. They include *Banksia occidentalis* (red swamp banksia), *B. robur* (swamp banksia), *B. integrifolia* (coast banksia), *Grevillea barklyana* (gully grevillea), *G. brachystylis*, *Hakea sericea*, *Mimetes hirtus* and a few others.

pH

This is the unit of measure for the acidity or alkalinity of soil and water. A neutral reading on this scale is pH7, with lower figures than this indicating increasing acidity and higher figures increasing alkalinity. In summary it is safe to say that most proteas prefer acid soils of pH 3.5–6.5. A few notable exceptions occur in slightly alkaline soils of around pH 7.5 – for example, *Protea obtusifolia* and *Protea repens* – but these grow equally well in mildly acid soils. Some races of the king protea, *P. cynaroides*, are found growing naturally in soils of pH 3.5, which ranks among the most acidic conditions that any plant can tolerate.

Water

There is a widespread belief that because proteas are dry-climate plants, they don't like water and should be kept dry. This is a certain recipe for disaster, because there is a crucial difference between 'dry' and 'well drained'. These plants do appreciate water – many commercial growers irrigate over the main growing periods to promote longer stems. The more free-draining the soil, the more necessary it is to irrigate (heavier soils will retain moisture longer and require less water in dry periods. Young plants also will require more water in the first summer after planting to ensure their successful establishment.

Some proteas, especially those that originate from relatively arid habitats, will certainly tolerate extended dry periods once they have become well established in the garden, but even these will produce larger flowers and more luxuriant growth when watered well.

Watering is best done on cooler days or during the evening, when there is less evaporation and the plants get the most benefit.

Nutrient requirements

Most members of the Proteaceae grow in soils that are low in nutrients and therefore are likely to be harmed through the application of fertilisers, especially the high phosphate content of 'general' fertilisers. Where proteas are obviously struggling in very poor soils or are being grown in tubs, the low-phosphate, slow-release granular fertilisers formulated for proteaceous plants can be used to advantage. Instructions regarding quantity should be carefully followed. They should be applied during the main growth periods, in spring and autumn.

In some instances, particularly with commercial flower growing, nitrogen in the form of ammonium sulphate or urea can be beneficial, and this is applied

SUMMARY OF PLANTING REQUIREMENTS

- Free-draining soils where waterlogging cannot occur.
- Soils that are basically low in nutrient content. In general, fertilisers should not have been used where planting is planned.
- Water should be available and applied in the first summer after planting and thereafter during prolonged dry periods.
- Sunny, open positions are generally favoured.
- Avoid overcrowding and 'cramming' among other plants.

three times a year from early spring at two-month intervals. In a normal home-garden situation, however, this is not usually necessary.

Planting positions

Most proteas will become healthier plants and produce more flowers of brighter colour if they are grown in a sunny position. There are always exceptions, and some species that in nature grow on south-facing slopes (Southern Hemisphere) will accordingly grow happily in positions receiving sun for only part of the day

A mixed planting of proteas and leucospermums provides a colourful early-summer display in this garden.

during summer and little direct sun during winter.

Most species do not like overcrowding, preferring good air circulation. Where this is lacking, bushes tend to become drawn up, spindly, unsightly and prone to infection by fungal diseases. This is particularly so in areas with warm, humid climates, where planting sites need to be selected that have as much air movement as possible in summer.

Try to position the plants in raised parts of the garden or on sunny slopes. Dips and hollows should be avoided, as both water and cold air accumulate there and frost is more likely to lie.

SITE PREPARATION

Ensure that the planting site is as free as possible of persistent weeds. Deeply rooted, strong-growing weeds and grasses will compete for nutrients with the surface-feeding roots of proteas and may create an unhealthy cramped and humid environment.

Planting may be done at any time of the year, especially with the freedom that the advent of container growing has given us. However, planting over summer will require extra watering to ensure survival. There are two preferable times for planting, dictated largely by climate.

In cooler regions, it is best to plant in spring when the heaviest frosts are over. This gives plants a chance to establish and acclimatise and, most importantly, to get to a reasonable size before the onset of winter. Additionally, plants have a chance to harden-up their autumn growth before frosts occur. Spring planting will mean summer watering will become important to the new plants.

In milder regions, the optimum time is undoubtedly autumn and winter. This enables plants to get their roots settled and spreading out into the surrounding soil before the dryness of summer arrives. Planting at this time will obviously mean less summer watering. Losses seem to be fewer among plants established over winter, so this is certainly the best planting time.

When planting young proteas, basic commonsense procedures that apply to most plants should be followed. Don't be tempted to use a post-hole borer, as this can glaze the sides of the hole and prevent root penetration. Dig a planting hole approximately twice the size of the planter bag or pot and then backfill with the loosened soil. This enables the roots to spread easily into the surrounding soil, ensure a firm anchorage and

rapidly provide moisture and nutrients, resulting in a healthy plant.

Unless the soil is very moist, it will pay to water in well at planting time and and repeat at least weekly, particularly in dry weather.

Newly planted larger specimens will require staking against high winds. Drive the stake in at an angle away from the trunk so root damage is minimised. To secure the plant to the stake, select soft materials that 'breathe', such as stockings or the commercially available foam-covered ties. As soon as the plants are stabilised and rooted into the surrounding soil, stakes should be removed to enable the plant to naturally develop the support it requires.

The ideal situation is to plant smaller-grade shrubs that establish themselves and bush up quickly so that they probably won't require staking at all. Large smooth rocks can be placed against the trunks of young plants to stop rocking movements in high winds. This has the added benefit of keeping the soil cool and acting to some extent as a mulch.

WEED CONTROL

In heavier soils where organic matter is high it is usually safe to use systemic herbicides applied carefully. Prolonged usage may build up enough residue in the soil to cause plant damage, particularly in lighter, porous soil low in organic material.

Weed matting (woven PVC film) allows water and air to pass through while suppressing weeds. The edges of the film should be either pinned down or buried to prevent it blowing away in the wind. It is more effective if covered with coarse bark chips, which are also more aesthetically pleasing, help keep the soil cool and take years to break down.

Avoid natural mulches such as grass clippings, sawdust, finely chopped bark, oak leaves and similar items because, as they rot down, they draw nitrogen from the soil, and they may harbour fungal diseases. Topdressing with nitrogenous fertilisers will counter some of these effects but also accelerates the rotting process of the mulch and may cause excessive soft, sappy growth.

Gardeners with good numbers of well-established proteas and access to a shredder can create a marvellously natural mulch of shredded material using old protea branches, prunings and dead flower heads, as these break down to form a natural upper soil layer in which the proteoid rootlets feed.

For some gardeners the ideal natural mulch will often be the most simple of all: having a lawn growing almost up to the plants. This keeps the soil cool and undisturbed, and provides a natural appearance. Remember to keep lawn fertilisers, which contain high levels of phosphate, well back from the root area of the bushes.

FROST

It is difficult to give clear-cut advice on proteas and frost. Generalisations are hazardous because seasonal variations are such in many parts of the world where the growing of proteas is borderline that plants may have been grown for several years with minimal or no frost damage, and yet a severe winter can wipe out a large range of species and cultivars. I would advise against commercial protea growing in districts with marginal climates.

When choosing plants for cool-climate gardens, pick those that grow naturally in similar conditions. The mountain-dwelling species of South Africa's Cape, such as *Protea venusta* and *P. subvestita*, tolerate frost with relative ease, and many species of *Leucadendron*, especially some of the *L. salignum* species and cultivars, can withstand quite heavy frosts. Some lower-growing *Protea* species such as *P. amplexicaulis*, *P. effusa* and *P. sulphurea* can be covered by snow for a few days without any adverse effect. The eastern Australian banksias such as *B. integrifolia* and *B. ericifolia* are far more tolerant of both heavy frost and variable soil types than the more spectacular West Australian species such as *B. hookeriana* and *B. ashbyii*, which tolerate only the lightest of frosts and require particularly well-drained soil.

Plants growing in good soils and producing lush growth are most susceptible to frost, while plants growing slowly in hard conditions are much tougher and more resistant to cold snaps. The sayings 'Grow them hard and watch them survive' and 'If they grow fast, they die fast' are appropriate.

Gardeners determined to grow the more tender species and cultivars in areas with colder winters should be aware that it is the first two years after planting out that are critical. Once a plant has some size, has a fair proportion of older hard wood and has acclimatised, its chance of surviving frost is greatly increased.

Protection over the first two winters is crucial and can be achieved, first, by planting in a sheltered position: in the lee of trees or against the sunny wall of a

Protea venusta is one of the more frost-hardy proteas, originating from altitudes of 2000 m, where light snowfalls are commonplace in winter.

house where the eaves offer shelter. Second, cover the young plants at night if frost threatens. A large corrugated cardboard carton is ideal. Only cover the plant at night, so it can harden up in the open during the day. In this way a more natural growth situation is created.

Where this type of 'spot' protection is impossible, it is better to use shade cloth, hessian or 'frost cloth' suspended on stakes rather than have any solid, impermeable material such as polythene film over the plant.

Plant in a position that avoids early-morning sun, to reduce the magnifying effect of the sun's rays on frost lying upon plants. Similarly, hosing frost off plants before the sun reaches them will reduce damage. Regular watering to ensure turgid foliage also helps.

PRUNING

Pruning proteas is simpler than often supposed, but does need to be done properly. Basic guidelines should be followed to keep them looking good and flowering prolifically.

Banksia
Some banksias have lignotubers (fire-resistant rootstocks) that enable them to regenerate, so they may be pruned vigorously. Examples include *B. attenuata*, *B. candolleana*, *B. menziesii* and *B. robur*. *Banksia integrifolia*, the coast banksia, while not possessing a lignotuber, can be pruned back severely, especially while young, and will produce masses of new growth. Most other banksias will require more cautious trimming if new growth is to be achieved. Staying within the current

season's growth with older specimens is the safe approach. Prune a little harder when the shrub is young, to promote a bushy habit. Remove spent flowers and cones to promote vigorous new growth.

Grevillea

As with banksias, grevilleas vary in the amount of pruning needed for different species and cultivars. However, most will be found to require little pruning except to shape them to individual requirements. Exceptions are more vigorous cultivars such as some of the ground-cover hybrids – e.g. 'Aussie Crawl', 'Fanfare', *G.* x *gaudichaudii*, 'Bronze Rambler' and 'Royal Mantle' – which can be cut back quite drastically to keep within bounds and promote thicker growth.

In the bushy, more tropical types such as 'Robyn Gordon', 'Superb', 'Misty Pink' and 'Golden Lyre', older plants that may have got out of hand or become 'leggy' can be brought back to tidy habits through hard pruning. 'Robyn Gordon' will regenerate magnificently from a stump.

Leucadendron

Most species need to be well pruned when the bracts have lost their colour and before new growth commences (usually early to late spring). Those with persistent rootstocks such as *Leucadendron salignum* and its many cultivars, including 'Safari Sunset' and 'Inca Gold', may be severely pruned back to almost a stump as soon as they deteriorate and become 'leggy'. This has the effect of virtual regeneration through the production of vigorous and bushy new growth from the base of the plant. In fact they should be pruned yearly to maintain a vigorous, long-stemmed bush.

Many other species that do not have a rootstock will need a light annual pruning to encourage a well-shaped, bushy habit. Heavy picking of bushes, whether for use in home floral arrangements or for commercial markets, is one of the best forms of pruning. Unpruned bushes, especially female forms, will produce short, less usable growths around the seed cone. Prostrate forms usually need just a light trimming to remove seed cones. The tallest species, *Leucadendron argenteum* (the Cape silver tree), will not attain its true majesty and natural height if it is pruned, though commercial growers do cut back this species hard to manage it for harvest.

Leucospermum

As a general rule, leucospermums need very little pruning in the home-garden situation, just some shaping to suit individual requirements. Flowers normally dead-head themselves after a while, but these can be removed earlier.

Only in the few cases where a persistent rootstock is present (e.g. *Leucospermum cuneiforme* and its cultivars) can they be hard pruned into the old wood. Other species should not be pruned far back into the previous year's growth, as they may not shoot again, especially with older bushes.

Mimetes

Species in this genus have a persistent rootstock and should be pruned back to a stump when they deteriorate with age to the woody or 'leggy' stage. They normally spring away into vigorous new growth from the base. Regular summer–autumn pruning coupled with picking will normally be enough to keep mimetes bushes compact.

Protea

Pruning will vary according to species, but only a very few may be safely hard pruned back to old wood. Such an example is *Protea cynaroides*, which has a ligno-tuberous rootstock and will even produce vigorous new growth from a stump.

Most other species may be lightly pruned to shape, but this should be confined to the previous year's growth. As a general guide, leave vigorous, healthy leaf growth below any cuts. Most plants are best shaped to form a well-branched, bushy form at an early age, before they become 'leggy' and sparsely branched and bare at the base. Even tip-pruning year-old plants will promote

This mature, well-maintained leucadendron exhibits the dense habit that results from annual pruning.

A young plant of *Protea cynaroides* showing the vigorous new growth promoted by hard pruning from an early age. Creating a good framework of branches from a low point on the plant will help to keep it compact and bushy .

branching. Taking the flower heads on long stems for floral work is a pleasurable way of pruning.

Spent flower heads of all species should be removed to encourage more vigorous new growth and better-looking shrubs. If possible, cut most of the current season's growth off with the dead flowers to keep new shoots low down in the bush, thereby promoting a compact habit. Untidy, spindly, downwards-facing branches should be removed flush with the trunk.

Serruria

Serrurias, especially *S. florida* and cultivars such as 'Sugar 'n' Spice' and 'Carmen', should be pruned back immediately after flowering, particularly while young, to encourage a well-branched, bushy habit. Otherwise they quickly become straggly and untidy.

Telopea (waratah)

It is essential with this genus to prune hard each year immediately after flowering and before new growth commences. This is because new shoots mainly develop within the flower head, so unpruned bushes will keep growing upwards instead of bushing out.

Very hard pruning, with removal of virtually the entire flowering stem, encourages multiple growing shoots from lower within the bush, resulting in a compact, bushy habit and far more flowering stems next season. Some commercial waratah growers have even been known to take to mature bushes with chainsaws to promote maximum regeneration!

PESTS AND DISEASES

In nature, particularly in South Africa, the Proteaceae are prone to a multitude of pests, and commercial monoculture demands strict control measures. In many other countries, where natural predators of proteas are not normally present, gardeners have almost no pest and disease problems. However, with international flower markets demanding perfect blooms that are totally free of any signs of pest and disease, regular, strict spray regimes have become a way of life for commercial protea flower growers.

The home gardener may never have to worry about spraying, apart from countering occasional caterpillar attacks on the tastier leucadendrons or some scale insects on proteas and waratahs. In most cases the usual sprays recommended by garden centres are effective.

Scale insects can be more persistent and often require the application of a mixture of a good insecticide plus an all-seasons spraying oil. Scale is easily recognisable: it is usually, white, black or brown and is shaped as a round lump (or pointed, mussel-shaped and white in the case of waratah scale). It attaches itself in limpet fashion to the underside of the leaf, but in severe infestations may occur all over a plant, including stems.

An infestation of white scale insect on the underside of New South Wales waratah (*Telopea speciosissima*) leaves.

A relatively new disease of proteas is *Elsinoe* scab, a fungus that has been observed to infect a wide range of them in South Africa, Australia and New Zealand. Of greater economic concern to commercial growers than to home gardeners, it produces scabby lesions on stems in particular, sometimes so severe that the stems are twisted and shrunken. The worst time for infection is

19

Leucospermum 'Firefly' displaying Elsinoe scab infection.

during humid conditions in spring and summer. Certain conditions favour the spread of the disease, notably excessively shaded situations and the splashing caused by overhead irrigation.

Infected stems should be cut hard back and the prunings burnt. Spraying with fungicides should be carried out. Octave, Bravo, Tilt and Benlate (benomyl) are some that have been found to be effective. Generally it is the systemic fungicides that are most effective, and commercial growers are well advised to carry out preventative spraying programmes. In South Africa considerable research is being undertaken on the *Elsinoe* problem and, in the case of *Leucospermum* cultivars, it has been found that *L. cordifolium* cultivars are very susceptible to infection, while *L. patersonii* and the cultivar 'High Gold' are extremely resistant. This suggests that the selection of resistant cultivars is rapidly going to become of prime importance to the industry.

Proteas are susceptible to *Phytophthora cinnamomi*, a soil-borne fungus disease that causes root rot and collapse of a number of types of plants, often in poorly drained soils, where it can spread downhill with the movement of water. This is a difficult fungus to control or eradicate, and commercial growers use systemic fungicides and soil drenches to help control the problem. It may be best advised to replant in well-drained sites away from infected areas (not downhill).

Good nurserymen, garden centres and horticultural companies should be able to advise on brands of spray chemicals available in particular markets, as these do vary from one country to another. It should be remembered that a more environmentally aware world has resulted in safer sprays being available and these should always be tried first.

PROPAGATION

The propagation of members of the Proteaceae can be difficult, and the most frustrating aspect is that the degree of difficulty can vary between closely related species and even cultivars of the same species. This becomes very significant when evaluating new cultivars, and ease of propagation can frequently determine how worthwhile it is to persevere with the development, naming and marketing of a new protea.

There are four methods of propagation:

Vegetative propagation

This is the most favoured method, using cuttings to produce an identical plant to the parent – an especially important feature when dealing with hybrids and variants, which have become so important to commercial growers and gardeners alike. Cultivars must be propagated from cuttings to ensure they are true to the parent plant. Seedlings, by comparison, will often produce considerable variation – and just occasionally they may even prove superior to the parent. Almost never will they give an identical plant to a hybrid one.

Cuttings are usually taken in either late spring or early autumn when new growth has advanced to the semi-hardwood stage. Timing can vary with the season, but generally material that has good 'whip' is selected: soft, new growth that has begun to harden up prior to summer or winter but still has good flexibility.

Sections of terminal or subterminal growth about 100–150 mm long are selected. The foliage on the lower third of the stem is removed carefully and the cut end is dipped in a root-forming hormone, indolebutyric acid (IBA), which may be either in powder or liquid form. With the liquid IBA, rates vary from 2000 ppm to 8000 ppm, depending on the species and type of material (4000 ppm appears to be the widely used dilution rate). With the powder, the strength used is what is generally referred to as 'No. 2' – for semi-hardwood cuttings. Cuttings are then firmed into a sterile rooting medium such as 50/50 peat and fine polystyrene, perlite or pumice; pure, finely granulated pumice or perlite; or a mixture of coarse, washed river sand with any of the above-mentioned ingredients. Ratios will vary according to individual preferences and experience. The trays or tubes of cuttings are then kept in a sheltered environment such as a shadehouse or cool glasshouse, where they are misted frequently to prevent the foliage from drying out. Excessively hot and humid glasshouse conditions are likely to cause 'damping off' of the cuttings through fungal infection, and should be avoided. Spraying with a suitable fungicide may be necessary. The 'open shade' situation, where good air circulation is provided, is often preferred. Rooting time varies from two or three weeks to months in some cases.

Well-rooted cuttings are carefully transplanted into large tubes, pots or smaller-sized planter bags. After an establishment period to permit roots to move out and fill their new environment, they are either planted out, moved to the next-size-up container or sometimes sold at that stage. Planting out to an open-ground position will usually occur in late autumn or winter in mild climates, or spring in cooler locations.

Seed

Some protea species have seeds that retain viability for many years, especially seeds with hard outer coatings. In general, however, the fresher the seed the quicker it is to germinate and the higher the rate of success. The natural time for sowing is in the autumn, and this fits

ABOVE: A well-rooted cutting ready for transplanting into a larger tube or small pot or planter bag.

BELOW: Young protea plants being grown-on under shade in an Australian wholesale nursery.

Leucadendron cone and seeds.

Grevillea 'Red Ruby' as a standard grafted onto a *G. robusta* rootstock.

spermum the cutting-graft technique has proved very successful, although the more traditional wedge grafting is also widely used.

Grafting is also used to create effective weeping standards. Taller, vigorous species such as *Grevillea robusta* are sometimes used as standardising rootstocks for prostrate grevilleas. *Banksia integrifolia* is used as a rootstock for disease-prone or difficult *Banksia* species to give more reliability under cultivation.

Leucospermum cuneiforme is used as a rootstock for grafting difficult or endangered South African species onto, examples being *Orothamnus zeyheri* (the rare and endangered marsh rose) and some *Mimetes* species.

the cycles of most proteas. Seedlings may be pricked out and moved into tubes in late winter or early spring.

To encourage germination and break the dormancy of some seeds, soak them in warm water. With some more difficult species, soaking in a 1 per cent solution of hydrogen peroxide for 24 hours is effective.

Seeds should be sown in a free-draining but moisture-retaining medium. Various mixtures of materials such as leaf mould, peat, coarse sand and pumice are used, and the seed is only lightly covered – never by more than the depth of the seed is a rule of thumb.

Seedlings are carefully transplanted into individual small pots or tubes in the early spring, being pricked out after the first set of true leaves has developed.

Grafting and budding

These techniques are not widely used with the Proteaceae. However, where a particular plant is difficult to establish, perhaps because it is pH-sensitive or susceptibile to root disease, it may be grafted onto a hardy, disease-resistant rootstock. Various types of grafting techniques are used. With *Grevillea* and *Leuco-*

Tissue culture

Also known as micro-propagation, this laboratory technique of taking tiny pieces from the growing tips of plants and multiplying them in a sterile solution, thus producing large numbers of identical plants, is used with many plants. As a fast-track way of very rapidly bulking up new cultivars this method has no peer. However, to date success has been limited to some Australian genera of the Proteaceae such as *Grevillea*, *Telopea* and *Isopogon*. While a number of others, such as *Leucospermum*, have shown promise, there are still problems to overcome with low rooting percentages. When this propagation method becomes the norm for the protea family (which is just a matter of time), there will be a virtual explosion of spectacular hybrids.

22

Proteas in the garden

BANKS, WALLS AND GROUNDCOVER

Increasingly it seems that gardens are becoming smaller and more demanding for landscape planning. City suburban sections are often steep, cut into hillsides; retaining walls are prominent. Home-owners have less time for gardening, with many other demands on their free time. They require an attractive garden to complement their lifestyle, but they want it easy-care, maintenance-free and effective.

Whether the situation calls for covering an unsightly clay bank, establishing dense groundcover on a difficult site, softening the hard lines of retaining walls or something to spill over low walls, there are numerous proteas to fill the position.

A few suggestions follow. Note that there are always overlapping uses, some groundcovers also being very suitable for banks and walls.

Dense, medium-height bank cover
Banksia candolleana – 1 m high x 2 m+ wide
Banksia spinulosa 'Collina Dwarf' – 1.5 x 2.5 m
Protea venusta – 1 x 2–3 m

Grevillea x *gaudichaudii* spreads and mounds handsomely in an establishing rock garden.

Banksia spinulosa 'Collina Dwarf' will form a dense, spreading shrub of 1.2 m high by 2–3 m wide.

Low groundcover
Banksia blechnifolia
Banksia integrifolia Austraflora 'Roller Coaster'
   (syn. 'prostrate')
Banksia serrata 'Pygmy Possum'
Grevillea 'Aussie Crawl'
Grevillea 'Bronze Rambler'
Grevillea fasciculata
Grevillea 'Fanfare'
Grevillea x *gaudichaudii*
Grevillea lanigera 'Mount Tamboritha'
Grevillea 'Royal Mantle'
Grevillea thelemanniana
Leucadendron salignum 'incisum'
Leucadendron salignum 'Red Carpet'

Leucospermum prostratum 'Groundfire'
Leucospermum prostratum 'Thompson's Gift'
Protea acaulos
Protea 'Joey'
Protea sulphurea

Retaining walls
Grevillea depauperata 'Orange Glow'
Grevillea fasciculata
Grevillea x *gaudichaudii*
Grevillea 'Royal Mantle'
Grevillea thelemanniana
Protea amplexicaulis
Protea sulphurea

Low walls
Banksia spinulosa 'Birthday Candles'
Leucospermum 'Thompson's Gift'
Protea acaulos
Protea 'Joey'

Grevillea 'Royal Mantle', a vigorous hybrid similar to 'Fanfare', cascades with great enthusiasm over a retaining wall, providing dense cover and a colourful display.

THE SHRUB GARDEN

Whether used in ornamental shrub borders or as feature garden subjects on their own, proteas have few equals for the variety of foliage form and colour, length of flowering over all the seasons and amazing range of growth habit. They must surely be a landscaper's dream come true!

For a border or boundary planting, imagine using a mix of taller-growing species for both background and shelter: for example, *Leucadendron argenteum*, the Cape silver tree, with its incredible shimmering foliage, plus the ferny-leaved *Grevillea robusta* (silky oak), with its spectacular large golden-orange flowers from late spring into summer. The brilliant scarlet flowers of *Embothrium coccineum*, the Chilean fire bush, offer vibrant spring colour, and the hardy and vigorous *Banksia integrifolia* provides nectar for birds over late summer into winter. All four grow to heights varying from 4 to 8 m and provide contrasting colour and form of foliage, as well as flowering at different times to provide continuity through the year. Alternatively, the mass-planting approach can be taken, using just one of these suggestions to give continuity of form and colour as a background.

Forward of this, the medium foreground planting can then be graduated down in height through medium-sized species and cultivars. Again, the massed but geometric approach can be taken by using just one species or variety planted in a row, or alternatively the approach may be to use great variety to give staggered flowering times and an assortment of leaf textures.

Protea amplexicaulis, here flanked by *P. recondita*, makes an unusual statement spilling over a stone retaining wall.

Protea acaulos is a good choice for spilling over low walls.

A range of leucadendrons and other proteas creates a colourful display in this rock garden.

A wide range of *Banksia, Leucadendron, Leucospermum, Protea, Grevillea* and other genera can be used, as it is in this height range of 1.5–2.5 m that there is the greatest selection to choose from.

The foreground can be kept to plants of restricted growth, the groundcover and low, mounding types. Here groundcover grevilleas such as 'Gaudichaudii', 'Aussie Crawl' and 'Fanfare' can be used to cover the ground rapidly and smother weed growth. Some lower shrubs in the 60–70 cm height range can still be used in this area for variety.

Overall, by having three distinct height areas within the planting, it is possible to view the entire border without any one plant obscuring those behind.

This type of planting plan can also be used to good effect in a circular garden, with the taller shrubs in the centre and progressively lower ones radiating outwards.

SCREENING

There are a number of broadly spreading shrubs in the Proteaceae that have excellent potential for quick and effective screening purposes. Whether it is to disguise an unsightly outbuilding, improve your privacy, block an unpleasant view of a neighbour's backyard, or for any of a number of other reasons, there is always a demand for shrubs suitable for screening. The main criteria are usually fast growth, wide, dense habits and, if possible, some attractive flowers and/or foliage as a bonus.

A great many grevilleas fulfil the requirements for fast, dense screening, and the following species and cultivars are worthy of consideration.

Grevillea x 'Audrey' – 2 m tall x 2 m wide; hardy, adaptable and attracts birds

Grevillea barklyana – to 8 m tall; fast, dense and broad; can be pruned

Grevillea 'Canberra Gem' – 2.5 x 2.5 m; vigorous and dense; also suitable as hedging; easily grown

Grevillea x 'Clearview David' – 2.5 x 2.5 m; dense, vigorous habit; attracts birds

Grevillea hookeriana 'hybrid' (syn. *Grevillea* 'Robin Hood') – 3 x 3 m; dense

Grevillea 'Ivanhoe' – 3 x 4 m; vigorous and dense; ideal screening and shelter

Grevillea x 'Merinda Gordon' – 2 x 2 m; a hardy, prickly cultivar

Grevillea x 'Poorinda Anticipation' – 2 x 2.5 m; broad habit

Grevillea x 'Poorinda Blondie' – 4 x 5 m; large,

vigorous and fast screening; can be pruned

Grevillea x 'Poorinda Constance' – 4 x 4 m; vigorous and hardy; may be pruned

Grevillea x 'Poorinda Peter' – 3 x 4 m; hardy and reliable; pickable foliage

Grevillea 'White Wings' – 3 x 6 m+; hardy and reliable; easily grown.

Several hakea are also suitable screening subjects:

Hakea laurina – 5 m high x 3 m wide; dense, bushy habit; appealing 'pincushion' flowers; prune to desired shape

Hakea salicifolia 'Gold Medal' – 5 x 3 m; broad growth habit; surprisingly hardy; variegated cream-and-green foliage; pink young growth

Leucadendron cultivars such as those with *L. xanthoconus* parentage (e.g. 'Patea Gold') and *L. salignum* cultivars such as 'Brook's Red' and 'Big Red' make excellent screen plants with their dense, broadly spreading habit. Certain other *Leucadendron* species, if regularly pruned, also develop a broader and denser habit.

Although not often thought of as likely screening plants, the larger *Leucospermum* species such as *L. reflexum* have considerable potential, especially in sandy coastal gardens subject to salt-laden wind. The dense grey-green foliage and colourful flowers over summer on a bush as large as 3 x 3 m provide an arresting display as well as an effective screen.

Some of the *Telopea* cultivars, mainly those with *T. oreades* parentage such as 'Burgundy', can make excellent fast-growing screening and hedging subjects. They can be pruned to the desired height or shape and produce spectacular displays of blooms in early spring.

A number of larger *Protea* species can be also used successfully to screen unwanted views. *Protea aurea*, bushier cultivars of *P. neriifolia*, *P. repens* and *P. roupelliae* are all possibilities. They can reach 3 m in height with an equal spread. Pruning from an early age to create a bushy framework will help to broaden the plants and increase their density.

SHELTER

The proteas are not usually thought of as shelter plants, but there are a few good species for this use. One of the best for taller, robust shelter is *Banksia integrifolia*, the coast banksia. This hardy, fast-growing plant can reach 20 m or more, responds well to hard pruning, which will thicken and widen its growth habit, and above

A *Telopea* cultivar (*T. speciosissima* x *T. oreades*) used as a hedge to screen off an unwanted view.

all is very wind-tolerant (including salt-laden wind). *Banksia ericifolia*, *B. marginata*, *B. media*, *B. praemorsa* and *B. serrata* are also very suitable shelter subjects, although not as high or quite so wind-resistant.

Hakea salicifolia, especially its variegated cultivar 'Gold Medal', can make a colourful medium-sized shelter that can be clipped to shape and made into a hedge. It will form wind protection of up to 3 m high with a width of 2–2.5 m. Other hakeas also have good shelter potential.

Although not a long-term proposition, *Leucadendron argenteum*, the Cape silver tree, can make a stunning, fast-growing shelter or boundary planting that will last several years before needing replanting.

Grevillea robusta, the silky oak, is another taller-growing protea suitable for shelter purposes. It will tolerate some pruning and shaping.

ATTRACTING BIRDS

The ability of proteas to attract nectar-seeking birds is one of their greatest advantages. Many proteas are primarily bird-pollinated, and it is common to see the beaks and heads of birds covered in pollen that is being efficiently transferred between flowers. In fact, cross-pollination causes many natural hybrids. It is interesting to upend a flower head of a protea such as

Protea repens, a classic example of a nectar-rich protea.

P. repens over a saucer and see how much nectar drains out over an hour or two, graphically demonstrating what an excellent food source proteas are, especially over the winter months.

So many members of the Proteaceae are rich in nectar that it is really unnecessary to list them all. Protea, grevillea and many banksia are among the most obvious genera that have numerous examples.

SEASONAL COLOUR AND PICKING

Winter

It is undoubtedly the winter colour they provide, and their availability at that time, that puts so many species of Proteaceae at the top of the popularity stakes with gardeners and floral artists. Over winter, many gardens, even in more temperate regions, are inclined to be drab and colourless, so any plants with bright colour and long-lasting cut flowers become very desirable.

The following lists give flowering times and suggested uses for some of the great range of winter-blooming proteas.

Banksia coccinea – midwinter–late spring; picking
Banksia ericifolia –winter; picking; attracts birds
Banksia hookeriana – winter–summer; display and picking.
Banksia integrifolia – autumn–spring; shelter; attracts birds
Banksia media – autumn–winter; picking
Banksia menziesii – autumn–spring; picking
Banksia praemorsa – winter–spring; picking
Grevillea alpina species and cultivars
Grevillea 'Australflora McDonald Park' – winter–spring
Grevillea brachystylis 'Bushfire' – flowers most of year, but especially winter
Grevillea x 'Canberra Gem' – winter–spring; attracts birds
Grevillea x 'Clearview David' – winter–spring; attracts birds
Grevillea x 'Goldrush' – winter
Grevillea hookeriana 'hybrid' (syn. 'Robin Hood') – year-round display and picking; screening; medium shelter; attracts birds
Grevillea lanigera 'Mt Tamboritha' – winter; groundcover
Grevillea x 'Pink Surprise' – long period of display

Ornamental grasses contrast strikingly with the winter colour of *Leucadendron laureolum* 'Colin Lennox'.

Grevillea x 'Poorinda Constance' – winter–spring
Grevillea x 'Poorinda Leane' – winter–spring
Grevillea x 'Poorinda Rondeau' – winter–spring
Leucadendron 'Bell's Supreme' – picking
Leucadendron 'Inca Gold' – picking
Leucadendron 'Jester' and 'Safari Sunshine' – very similar cultivars with variegated foliage; picking
Leucadendron laureolum cultivars – winter–spring; picking
Leucadendron 'Maui Sunset' – winter–spring; picking
Leucadendron 'Red Gem' – autumn–winter; picking
Leucadendron 'Safari Sunset' – autumn–spring; superb picking
Leucadendron salignum (most cultivars) – winter–spring; picking
Leucadendron 'Silvan Red' – autumn–winter; picking
Leucadendron strobolinum and cultivars (e.g. 'Waterlily') – picking
Leucadendron 'Super Star' – winter–spring
Mimetes cucullatus – winter–spring; picking
Paranomus reflexus – picking
Protea aurea and cultivars – autumn–winter; screening
Protea 'Clark's Red' – year-round; attracts birds.
Protea compacta – year-round, especially winter; picking
Protea cynaroides (winter-flowering variants) – picking
Protea laurifolia (several cultivars) – year-round, especially winter; picking
Protea longifolia (variable) – winter–spring
Protea magnifica (winter-flowering variants) – picking; attracts birds

Protea nana – novelty winter–spring display
Protea neriifolia (numerous cultivars) – autumn–spring; picking; attracts birds
Protea obtusifolia – autumn–spring
Protea repens (various cultivars) – autumn–spring; attracts birds
Protea stokoei – picking
Protea sulphurea –some picking potential; bank/wall cover
Serruria florida – winter–spring; picking
Serruria 'Sugar 'n' Spice' – winter–spring; tub culture

Spring

During spring proteas tend to be overlooked in favour of more traditional flowers, which produce massed displays. However, if the garden is largely made up of shrubs and there is little emphasis on bulbs and blossom trees, then there is a range of proteaceous shrubs to choose from, as so many species and cultivars flower from late winter through the spring months. This is especially obvious in cooler climates, where plants that are winter-flowering in mild areas tend to bloom a

Leucadendron and *Protea* species mix naturally in this garden in a late-winter to early-spring seasonal overlap of texture and colour.

month or two later, in early spring. Because of this quite complex seasonal range, no specific suggestions are given for spring performers, but you can choose from those on the winter list above where 'winter–spring' is indicated, and 'spring–summer" from the summer list below. Very few species or cultivars flower just in the spring, as proteas have marvellously prolonged flowering periods. It is even possible to have, for instance, some *Protea magnifica* cultivars that start flowering in midwinter and others that will commence in mid-spring and carry on into midsummer.

The notable exception is the spectacular waratahs (*Telopea* species and cultivars), which are most decidedly spring-flowering shrubs.

Summer

Beyond doubt, the genus that stands out for brilliant summer colour is *Leucospermum*, whose 'pincushion' flower heads add immeasurably to summer gardens in milder areas. Other genera also provide summer colour and pickablity, and the following list suggests just some of the many outstanding species and cultivars.

Banksia burdettii – late spring–early autumn; excellent for home and commercial picking
Banksia occidentalis – summer–autumn; picking
Banksia prionotes – late summer–autumn; suitable for home and commercial picking
Banksia speciosa – summer–autumn; picking
Banksia victoriae – summer–autumn
Grevillea barklyana – spring–summer; picking; fast-growing screening
Grevillea hookeriana 'hybrid' ('Robin Hood') – year-round, especially spring–summer; screening
Grevillea 'Misty Pink' – year-round, especially summer
Grevillea 'Robyn Gordon' – year-round, especially spring–summer
Grevillea 'Superb' – year-round, especially spring–autumn
Many other *Grevillea* species and cultivars will also provide spectacular summer colour.
Leucospermum conocarpodendron (and cultivars) – late spring–summer; picking
Leucospermum cordifolium (many cultivars) – mid-spring–summer; picking
Leucospermum cuneiforme (and cultivars) – late spring–summer

Leucospermum lineare (and cultivars) – spring–summer; picking
Leucospermum reflexum and variety 'luteum'– late spring–summer; some picking potential
Protea aristata – late summer; sometimes picked despite pungent foliage
Protea cynaroides (summer-flowering variants) – picking
Protea grandiceps – late spring–summer; some picking potential
Protea roupelliae – late summer
Protea venusta – late summer–autumn; excellent bank and groundcover

RIGHT: *Leucospermum cuneiforme* provides a stunning contrast with *Bougainvillea* 'Scarlet O'Hara' in a townhouse summer garden.

Autumn

The summer list shows that many proteaceous plants extend their display into autumn, and it is amazing just how many of the species, although they have a peak flowering at other times, retain a few flowers at this time of year. Some seem never to stop flowering! Examples are *Protea* 'Clark's Red', some *Protea laurifolia* cultivars, *P.* 'Pink Ice' and some of the *P. neriifolia* hybrids.

The first of the red hybrid leucadendrons are beginning to produce colourful bracts by autumn, and often the brilliant 'Safari Sunset' is becoming pickable as its bracts firm. It is fair to say, however, that autumn is not such a prolific flowering time for the Proteaceae as the other seasons are. However, with careful selection it is possible to have year-round colour and picking from this versatile family of plants.

CUT FLOWERS

The proteas have legendary attributes as cut flowers. From their incredible vase life and their versatility in all styles of floral art, to their ability to travel long distances when shipped and 'bounce back' when unpacked, they have earnt a place in the hearts of both floral designers (amateur and professional) and commercial florists, not to mention the home gardener who can pop out into the garden at any time of the year to pick a few blooms for a quick and stylish arrangement.

To ensure a long vase life, always use clean containers and water. Add a commercial preservative to the water to further extend vase life, and remove foliage that would be under the water in the container. Place the flower arrangement in a cool part of the room, away from direct sunlight. Replace the water weekly and at the same time trim the ends of the stems. This will re-open the vessels that transport the water up the stems.

How cut protea flowers are displayed in arrangements depends on either the individual preference of the floral designer or the use to which they are to be put. In modern homes with clean 'minimalist' lines, often quite plain decors and strong architectural features, proteas can be used to striking effect (indeed they are sometimes referred to as 'architectural flowers' for their strong form). Sometimes a single flower head of the king protea in a clear glass vase will be ample decoration by itself in a room. For some floral artists a spectacular arrangement utilising a broad range of proteas

This spectacular arrangement captures the essence of proteas in floral art

– flowers, foliage and fruit – will be the approach. For example, tall, feathery leucadendron foliage and bracts can be used as 'backing material', with proteas, waratahs, banksias or leucospermums as the focus of the arrangement.

Ikebana flower arrangers can also use proteas to dramatic effect, and a few smaller species of proteas make delightful posies. At floral-art exhibitions, proteas may be seen used with often startling results: perched in the branches of dramatic driftwood arrangements, in glass bowls, or even wired up into extraordinary space-age creations.

OPPOSITE: *Protea cynaroides*, the king protea, used in simple style to make a striking architectural statement in a modern home.

ABOVE: A plantation of *Leucospermum cordifolium* nearly ready to pick provides an eye-catching sight.

BELOW: *Leucospermum reflexum* var. 'luteum' grown as a commercial cut-flower crop.

Commercial cultivation

Generations of home gardeners have known of the amazing longevity of cut protea blooms, the unique architectural form they possess that makes them so versatile in floral arrangements, and how easy they are to work with. Commercial flower growers, on the other hand, took until the mid-1980s to really appreciate the potential of proteaceous flowers. A handful of growers in South Africa and New Zealand quietly went about the business of selling protea flowers for decades before that, but momentum only gathered when flower markets in Europe, Japan and the United States realised this 'new' crop's potential. Today proteas are best known as commercial cut flowers.

Apart from the Cape region of South Africa and Australia, the main homes of proteas, they are now grown both in home gardens and in increasing quantities for commercial cut flowers in other such diverse localities as New Zealand, the United States (in coastal Southern California and parts of Hawaii – mainly the mountain slopes of Maui), Israel, Norfolk Island, the Canary Islands and Zimbabwe. Trial plantings showing some promise have also been carried out in the northern highlands of Thailand, south-west Portugal and the Madeira Islands. In the year 2000 Israel alone is reported to have exported some 28 million stems of *Leucadendron* 'Safari Sunset', a 10 per cent increase on the previous year. This leucadendron is also a major export crop in New Zealand (where it originated), Hawaii, Australia and other countries.

Some of the best markets for protea flowers are Japan, North America and Europe. Virtually without exception all markets demand perfect quality: straight stems of maximum length and blemish-free blooms (or bracts) at the perfect stage of development for both marketability and lasting qualities. Both in the marketplace and at point-of-entry agricultural inspections, any sign of pest or disease means instant rejection or fumigation (which may damage or even destroy the blooms).

Regular spray programmes have become a way of life for commercial protea growers to ensure the perfection that the market demands. Post-harvest treatment of flowers, usually involving rapid cooling to as low as 0°C, is becoming the norm. Humidity levels in cool

Main commercial protea-growing regions of the world.

rooms must be carefully monitored. 'Girdling', where a ring of bark and phloem is removed just below the flower head, has been found to delay the leaf-blackening problem to which many proteas are subject. Ongoing research into methods for further improving the longevity of cut blooms and finding better shipping methods is being carried out. Packaging and marketing are also being constantly improved, and airlines provide more space for fast world-wide shipment of flower consignments. In some countries exporters and co-operatives have even chartered their own aircraft.

Most forward-thinking protea growers also recognise that, while in the short term quality control and shipping methods are very important, in the long term it is the development of new and improved cultivars that holds the key to sustainable industry growth. As with so many crops, breeding resistance to pests and dis-

Leucadendron 'Safari Sunset' is the most widely grown of the proteas for cut-flower purposes.

eases, the ability to reach market destinations in prime condition, and keeping one step ahead of competitors with better colours and new and different hybrids are vital to the industry.

Enterprising horticulturists strive to select plants grown from seed that show significant improvements over the parent plant. Many natural hybrids of striking quality have been been introduced to cultivation in this manner, but it is in the field of artificially manipulated hybrids that the greatest potential is shown. While to date only a relative handful of these hybrids have been commercialised, they indicate where the future lies.

The first and most outstanding example of a manipulated hybrid is the New Zealand-raised *Leucadendron* 'Safari Sunset', which resulted from work carried out in the early 1960s by Ian Bell of Wanganui. He was carrying on work started by his mother-in-law, Jean Stevens, and used *L. laureolum* and *L. salignum* (red form) for his pioneering hybridising work. He was attempting to produce a red version of the *L. laureolum*, which normally has long-stemmed yellow bracts. Some of the most exciting work with the genus *Protea* has been carried out by scientists at the Fynbos Research Unit at Elsinburg in South Africa. Some of these hybrids have been released to the industry there, including:

'Sheila' (*P. magnifica* x *P. burchellii*)
'Venetia' (*P. magnifica* x *P. neriifolia*)
'Pink Duke' (*P. compacta* x *P. susannae*)
'Candida' (*P. magnifica* x *P. obtusifolia*)
'Valentine' (*P. cynaroides* x *P. compacta*)
'King Grand' (*P. cynaroides* x *P. grandiceps*)
'Venus' (*P. repens* x *P. aristata*)
'Liebencherry' (*P. repens* x *P. longifolia*)
Unnamed (*P. cynaroides* x *P. nitida*)
Unnamed (*P. cynaroides* x *P. repens*)

Also originating from South Africa during the mid-1990s is the important *Leucadendron* hybrid 'Rosette' (*L. laureolum* x *L. elimense* subsp. *salteri*), which is particularly productive, possibly even more profuse than the famous 'Safari Sunset'. It produces numerous long green-to-yellow stems.

Very significant work is also being carried out by the University of Hawaii at Maui, notably in selecting and breeding for disease resistance. Work with *Leucospermum*, for instance, is resulting in *Elsinoe* scab-resistant hybrids. The advanced hybrid 'Rachel', (*L. lineare* x *L. vestitum*) x *L. glabrum*, is a prime example, while other selections are proving resistant to *Botrytis* and *Drechslera*. Research also involves breeding and selecting early-flowering *Leucospermum* cultivars.

The University of Adelaide in South Australia has also conducted a breeding and selection programme for the commercial flower industry, with the emphasis on their native *Banksia*. This has resulted in some excellent 'Waite' cultivars being released to the industry.

Some of the major Proteaceae species and cultivars being grown in volume by commercial flower growers for export are:

Banksia species and cultivars, including *B. ashbyii, B. baxteri, B. burdettii, B. coccinea* (including selections such as 'Waite Crimson' and 'Waite Flame'), *B. hookeriana, B. menziesii, B. prionotes, B.* 'Waite Orange' (*B. hookeriana* x *B. prionotes*) and *B. victoriae*.

Leucadendron argenteum (cones and foliage), *L.* 'Pisa', *L. laureolum* cultivars, *L.* 'Safari Sunset', *L. xanthoconus* cultivars, and an ever-increasing number of newer examples.

Leucospermum species and cultivars, particularly some of the *L. cordifolium, L. conocarpodendron, L. glabrum, L. linaere* and *L. patersonii* cultivars.

Protea species and cultivars, including *P. cynaroides, P. magnifica, P.* 'Pink Ice', and a number of newer

ABOVE: A young commercial planting of *Leucospermum cordifolium* in an idylic coastal setting.

BELOW: Freshly picked *Leucospermum cordifolium* being conditioned for export.

cultivars, especially those with *P. magnifica* and *P. compacta* parentage.

Serruria florida (blushing bride)

Telopea speciosissima (New South Wales waratah) in a range of cultivars including white-flowered examples.

For home markets and floral art in countries where the plants are widely grown, the range of material that can be used is much broader and includes smaller-flowered types suitable for posy work, spray types for backing or fillers, and species with shorter vase life. The male-flowered leucadendrons, which may have insufficient vase life for export purposes, are often acceptable for local use.

It is intriguing to witness the increasing use of proteas in the television and movie industry, where bowls of protea blooms can be seen in the background as part of stage sets, sometimes blended with other exotic species such as bird-of-paradise flower (*Strelitzia*), *Heliconia* or ginger. Such dramatic displays indicate the international status the protea now holds as a high-value exotic flower.

DRIED FLOWERS

Banksias, proteas, serrurias and some leucadendrons are widely used in dried-flower arrangements. Much is still to be learned regarding the retention of colour. Normal air-drying techniques, with flowers hung upside down in a cool, dry, dark place, usually cause most of the colour to be lost. Some growers have found ways to retain colour using silica, but these are time-consuming and often closely guarded secrets. Another, unpleasant-smelling method is to burn sulphur in an enclosed situation with the flowers.

Freeze-drying is being perfected and can give some excellent results now that timing and other techniques have been fine-tuned. This is an expensive method, however, and many amateurs will carry on hanging blooms upside down in cool, dry, dark rooms, which will enable a reasonable degree of colour retention.

The female seed cones of *Leucadendron* species are used in long-lasting displays. The dominant cone used here is from *L. argenteum*, the Cape silver tree.

Leucadendron female cones, when fully mature, dry beautifully and are often used. Good examples are *L. argenteum*, *L. laureolum*, *L. tinctum* and *L. macowanii*. Sprays of the male flowers of *L. conicum*, if picked at the bud stage, will dry well, keeping their appealing steel-blue colour.

Leaves of *Banksia brownii*, *B. baxteri*, *B. grandis* and *B. speciosa* also dry easily and form the basis of many dried arrangements.

Fully dried flower heads of many *Protea* species, while often used complete, can also have their central flower mass removed to expose the highly ornamental seed receptacle. *P. neriifolia*, *P. magnifica* and *P. repens* are examples.

Identification

Species and cultivars illustrated and described in the following pages have been selected using various criteria, including botanical significance, representation of a particular genus, and plants that are likely to be available to gardeners and commercial growers either now or in the foreseeable future.

The coloured panels offer a summary of important features of each plant. **H** represents the height the subject is likely to attain under cultivation, while **F** indicates the usual flowering time.

ALLOXYON

This recently named genus is a division of *Oreocallis*, which itself originally resulted from a division of *Embothrium*. There are four species, three being native to north-eastern Australia and one to New Guinea.

All four species are noted as very ornamental trees with attractive flowers and timber that has been used commercially. The latter has given rise to common names such as red silky oak, pink silky oak, satin silky oak, etc., which leads to confusion with other genera such as *Darlingia* and *Grevillea*, both of which have species with 'silky oak' in the common names.

A. pinnatum is the best-known species under cultivation, hence it is the one described here. *A. flammeum* is another tall-growing species seen occasionally in warm-climate gardens, mainly in Queensland. It, too, produces scarlet-red blooms in spring and summer.

Alloxylon pinnatum

(Previously *Oreocallis pinnata* and *Embothrium wickhamii* var. *pinnata*)

Queensland tree waratah

This tall ornamental tree is usually found growing in the rainforests of Queensland and northern New South Wales. However, it can be cultivated successfully in many mild-climate gardens with well-drained, fertile soils and some protection from strong wind.

Alloxylon pinnatum is a handsome tree with spectacular red blooms that are proving suitable as commercial cut flowers.

This distinctive species develops a sturdy trunk and robust habit, eventually forming a dense canopy. Deep green glossy leaves, to 20 cm long, provide a foil for the rich red tubular flowers, which are profusely carried in dense terminal clusters from spring to early summer. They have been described as having an appearance midway between a grevillea and a waratah.

Alloxylon pinnatum is a very suitable subject for a specimen tree in many gardens, arousing attention and admiration. It is also becoming recognised as having excellent cut-flower potential, with a number of Australian growers succeeding with export of the lightweight blooms.

H: 15+ m	Attracts birds
F: Spring–early summer	Cut flowers
Frost-tender	

AULAX

There are are just three species of *Aulax*, all being native to the southern Cape in South Africa. They are characteristically erect in habit, vary in height from 1 to 2 m and have very distinctive male and female flowers borne on separate plants.

Aulax cancellata

(Previously *A. pinifolia*)

Apart from leucadendrons, *Aulax* is the only member of the South African Proteaceae with unisexual flowers borne on separate male and female plants. Australian nurseries market only the male plants of *A. cancellata*, whose colourful yellow catkins are produced during spring. In New Zealand it is the female plant that is in demand, with its long-lasting, deep red seed cones and appealing bronze-red needle-like young growth. Plants attain a height of 2 m if left unchecked, but are usually restricted to 1 m or less with regular pruning. These plants are well suited to container growing and make handsome tub subjects on a patio or deck. (It is important to use a suitable potting mix – see page 15.)

A. cancellata is relatively easy to grow, with requirements typical for the Proteaceae: free-draining, lighter soils; good air circulation; avoidance of high-phosphate

The colourful seed cones of *Aulax cancellata* persist for months.

fertilisers ; and a sunny aspect that is not prone to heavy frosts (though they can tolerate midwinter temperature drops to –5°C).

H: 2 m	Medium frost-hardy
F: Spring	Cut flowers

BANKSIA

Named in honour of Sir Joseph Banks, who collected the first banksia specimens during Captain Cook's 1770 voyage. One of the best-known and spectacular genera of the Australian Proteaceae, comprising 75 species, 13 naturally occurring varieties and several registered cultivars, the banksias occur through most of coastal Australia. The species occurring in Western Australia tend to be the most spectacular, producing vivid colours and are keenly sought after as cut flowers. Eastern species are generally hardier and easier to cultivate.

Growth habit ranges from prostrate (*B. repens* and *B. gardneri*) through dense, bushy shrubs to trees of 16 m high (*B. serrata* and *B. integrifolia*). Foliage may be small and heath-like (*B. ericifolia*) to spectacularly large, leathery and with deep triangular teeth (*B. grandis*). Flowers are generally in the form of cylindrical or acorn-shaped cones, and may be squat or elongated. Colour varies from silvery green through brilliant golds, yellows and orange to almost violet and flamboyant red shades. The size of these spectacular flower cones can range from the diminutive *B. meisneri*, at just 2–3 cm, to the 40 cm cones of *B. grandis*.

The fascinating buds and flowers of *Aulax cancellata*.

Banksias have been grown as a commercial cut-flower crop in Hawaii and Israel for many years, and more recently in Australia, where research to select improved forms and conduct breeding programmes is providing valuable support and opportunities for growers.

The representative range of the more readily obtainable *Banksia* species depicted in this book should provide inspiration to gardeners to grow this genus.

B. ashbyii, one of the 'acorn flower' types of banksia.

Banksia ashbyii

Ashby's banksia

This species bears large (to 15 cm long and 8 cm diameter) cylindrical flower heads of soft apricot-orange, which are carried terminally from late winter through spring, and even into summer in some localities. These are highly regarded cut flowers with an excellent vase life. Foliage is typically dense, with individual leaves up to 30 cm long and deeply serrated. Growth habit is variable, sometimes being of small-tree height (to 8 m), but more usually under cultivation reaching 2 m with a greater width.

A species that is not always easily grown outside its native Western Australia, *B. ashbyii* is nevertheless well worth attempting in milder climates with well-drained, lighter soil types. Success is more likely in districts with predominate winter rainfall and long dry summers.

H: 2–8 m	Tolerates light frosts
F: Late winter–summer	Cut flowers

Banksia attenuata

Coast banksia, slender banksia

The startlingly intense sulphur-yellow flower spikes of this species may reach 25 cm in length and are prominently displayed during spring and summer. In nature, varying forms occur, ranging from small trees to bushy shrubs. The latter is considered preferable for gardens. Because this species has a lignotuber, it may be severely pruned to encourage a more branched, bushy growth habit. The narrow, stiff leaves have grey undersides and are variable in length.

B. attenuata is grown as a cut-flower subject, particularly in its West Australian habitat, and it has good lasting qualities. Although tolerant of frost to –4°C, it generally is difficult to cultivate in humid conditions. It is adaptable to varying soil types and is noted for withstanding wind.

Photograph on page 40

H: 2–5 m	Attracts birds
F: Spring–summer	Cut flowers
Medium frost-hardy	

Banksia baueri

Possum banksia, woolly banksia, teddybear banksia

The common names of this species refer to its very large woolly flower cones, which, when both fresh and dead, give the appearance of furry animals perched among the foliage. These extraordinary blooms – the widest of any banksia species, at 15 cm and up to 20 cm long –

Huge flower cones perch like woolly animals among the branches of *Banksia baueri*.

are produced from autumn through winter and into spring. Colour ranges from an orange-brown form to a silver-grey shade.

Generally *B. baueri* is a compact shrub of 1.5 m in height, but under cultivation may reach 2 m. Leaves are usually up to 13 cm long and have serrated margins. While the flowers are neither long-stemmed nor brightly coloured, and therefore not 'commercial', they are often used in feature arrangements.

Tolerant of a wide range of soils (even mildly alkaline ones) provided they are free-draining, the possum banksia is frost-resistant to approximately –6°C and is generally wind-tolerant.

H: 1.5–2 m	Medium frost-hardy
F: Autumn–spring	

Banksia baxteri

Bird's nest banksia, Baxter's banksia

The squat, lime-green buds of the bird's nest banksia open to form globe-shaped yellow flowers atop long stems during late spring through summer to early autumn. A popular long-lasting cut flower that also dries well, *B. baxteri* is heavily picked for this purpose in its native Western Australia as well as in other parts of the world, notably Hawaii. The unique foliage is deeply serrated and, either fresh or dried, is also used for floral work . Mature shrubs are generally neat and erect, growing to a height of about 3 m.

Well-drained, lighter soils are essential to the successful cultivation of this species. It is frost-tolerant to around –5°C, withstands winds well and is adaptable to a range of climates.

H: 3 m	Medium frost-hardy
F: Late spring–early autumn	Attracts birds
	Cut flowers and foliage

Banksia blechnifolia

This versatile prostrate species from southern Western Australia gains its specific name from the similarity of the foliage to the *Blechnum* genus of ferns. The branched stems are carried on the soil surface and the handsome foliage is held erectly, up to 45 cm in height. A mature bush may cover an area of 4 m in diameter and, with a somewhat 'mounding' habit, may reach 75 cm high.

The striking 16 cm long cylindrical flower spikes appear in late spring and are well displayed at the ends of the branchlets. They are a rich pink shade in bud, opening to a light red with conspicuous yellow pollen displayed on freshly opened flowers.

Banksia baxteri, with its long stems and lasting qualities, is popular for both fresh and dried cut flowers.

LEFT: *Banksia attenuata* creates a striking picture.

B. blechnifolia is an attractive ground banksia.

41

B. blechnifolia is a splendid choice for a rock garden or planter, where the handsome leaves are a talking point year-round, and the spring flowers provide a bonus. The leaves can be dried for floral work. Plants can be lightly pruned at the branch forks to keep the habit compact. This reliable, trouble-free species prefers well-drained soils, sunny positions and is tolerant of frosts to about –5°C.

H: 70 cm	Medium frost-hardy
F: Late spring	

Banksia burdettii

Burdett's banksia, golden acorn, golden banksia

In nature this lovely Western Australia species usually forms a rounded bush up to 4 m high. In the home garden or commercial flower farm, however, it is rare to see specimens larger than 2–3 m.

The bright orange acorn-shaped flower heads open from silver-grey buds from late summer to autumn and may be 12 cm long and up to 10 cm wide when fully open. They are beautiful as a cut flower, both fresh and dried, and are a popular picking species in South Australia and Hawaii.

Well-drained lighter soils are preferred by this species, which is most successfully grown in areas with dry summers and winter rains. The occasional light frost is tolerated, and a sunny position is required. It should be lightly pruned after flowering.

H: 2–4 m	Attracts birds
F: Late summer–autumn	Cut flowers
Tolerates light frosts	

Banksia burdettii is an excellent cut-flower species.

Banksia coccinea

Albany banksia, scarlet banksia, waratah banksia

This is one of the more spectacular species and deservedly popular as a cut flower. The highly ornamental, squat, cylindrical flowers open from woolly grey buds and can vary in colour from bright orange through rich scarlet to almost crimson. The scarlet form is the most commonly seen. Blooms are produced on long sturdy stems from late winter to early summer with a spring peak. It is grown commercially for cut flowers in its native Western Australia, Hawaii, South Africa and in some parts of New Zealand.

Usually a narrowly erect shrub of some 3 m in height, regular pruning or hard picking can transform it into a densely branched shrub. Foliage is short and squat in appearance, leathery and lightly serrated with a grey underside.

B. coccinea is tolerant of light to medium frosts of –5°C, and requires well-drained, light or sandy soils, full sun and some shelter from heavy winds.

H: 3 m	Medium frost-hardy
F: Late winter–early	Attracts birds
summer	Cut flowers

Banksia ericifolia

Heath-leaved banksia, heath banksia

Probably the most adaptable and easily grown banksia species, *B. ericifolia* is widely cultivated in many parts of the world, including the UK, where it was first grown in 1788. It is grown successfully in both warm, humid environments and cold, dry climates. It is tolerant of salt-laden winds, will grow in mildly alkaline soils and is frost-hardy to –8°C or more. It is used as a windbreak or screening plant, is attractive to nectar-seeking birds and is grown for the cut-flower market in some parts of the world, such as Maui in Hawaii.

The long (up to 25 cm) cylindrical flower spikes are usually an orange-brown colour, are produced prolifically during autumn and winter, and have prominently hooked styles that open from the top of the spike. The small bright green leaves bear a superficial resemblance to plants of the *Erica* genus (heath), hence the botanical specific name and the common ones.

H: 5 m	Attracts birds
F: Autumn–winter	Cut flowers
Frost-hardy	

Banksia coccinea, the sensational scarlet banksia.

Banksia ericifolia is one of the most easily grown species.

B. ericifolia is usually a dense, bushy shrub of up to 5 m high with an almost equal width, but can be pruned lightly to maintain a smaller dimension. Care should be taken not to cut back into old wood, which will be shy to produce new growth.

Banksia gardneri

This prostrate species from southern Western Australia has a lignotuber and produces spreading branches at ground level to a metre or more in length. The erectly held leathery leaves may measure 40 cm in length and are thickly produced. The flower spikes are cylindrical in shape and may vary in colour from rusty brown to pink shades with the different varieties. They are produced at ground level, are held in upright groups and are normally seen over the spring months.

A slow-growing shrub well suited to rockeries and similar garden positions, B. gardneri is sometimes considered a connoisseur's or collector's item. Well-drained, lighter soil types are preferred by this species, which is adaptable to partial shade. Frosts to –6°C in conditions of normal rainfall are tolerated.

Photograph on page 44

H: 40 cm (foliage)	Medium frost-hardy
F: Spring	

Banksia gardneri is an intriguing ground species.

Banksia 'Giant Candles' is a large-flowered hybrid that is particularly vigorous and hardy.

Banksia 'Giant Candles'

This registered cultivar, believed to be a cross between *B. ericifolia* and *B. spinulosa*, is a naturally occurring hybrid from the east coast of Australia. It has the appearance of a large-flowered, vigorous form of *B. ericifolia*. The spectacular flower spikes can be 40 cm or more in length and are a deep orange-brown colour. They are produced throughout autumn, winter and into spring, and are sought after by nectar-seeking birds. Foliage is fine, dark green and very dense. Generally a large, dense shrub growing to 4 m, it is useful for screening and background purposes, or may be trimmed to form a specimen.

'Giant Candles' requires a reasonably well-drained soil and a sunny position. It is regarded as adaptable, being frost- and wind-tolerant and easily cultivated.

H: 4 m	Attracts birds
F: Autumn–spring	Cut flowers
Frost-hardy	

Banksia grandis

Bull banksia, giant banksia

This spectacular species is noteworthy for its foliage and its flowers. The leaves may be up to 50 cm long and are arguably the most dramatic of any *Banksia* species. They are a shining deep green with grey undersides, and are deeply divided, almost to the midrib, giving the appearance of large, jagged teeth. Young growth is particularly attractive, being pale bronze or red and soft and woolly. Mature leaves are often picked and dried for floral work.

The flower spikes, up to 40 cm long, are a sulphur-yellow shade and have the appearance of giant candles placed on the tree during the main flowering time of spring and early summer.

This is usually a sturdy tree of up to 10 m at maturity, but there are smaller-growing coastal variants with low, spreading habits. Native to the south-west of Western Australia, *B. grandis* requires free-draining soils, sun or partial shade, and is wind-tolerant in most situations. It can withstand midwinter temperature drops to as low as –4°C. However, it may be difficult for gardeners to establish in some localities.

H: 10 m	Medium frost-hardy
F: Spring–early summer	Attracts birds

RIGHT: *Banksia grandis* is dramatic with its huge yellow flower spikes, spectacular leaves and massive seed cones.

Banksia integrifolia

Coast banksia, white honeysuckle

The most common of the eastern Australia species, the coast banksia is distributed from Victoria to northern Queensland in varying forms.

The cylindrical flower spikes are 10 cm long and 6 cm wide when fully developed. The silvery-yellow blooms, produced from autumn through winter into spring, are prized by nectar-seeking birds.

Foliage is variable: juvenile leaves are usually broad and irregularly toothed, while mature leaves are smooth-margined (entire) and lanceolate in shape. They have white undersides that tend to give the tree a silvery appearance in wind.

Normally of vigorously erect growth habit to 25 m high, *B. integrifolia* can also be seen as a prostrate shrub, reaching to only 20 cm by 2 m or more wide. This form is ideal for groundcover in coastal gardens and is sold as either *B. integrifolia* 'prostrate' or *B.* 'Austraflora

ABOVE: The cones of the coast banksia shed seed freely, and seedlings are often found growing under the trees.

BELOW: This prostrate form of *B. integrifolia* is useful in coastal gardens, where it is unaffected by salt-laden winds.

Roller Coaster'. The more usual upright forms can be kept pruned and used as dense hedging, screening and taller shelter. A particularly wind-tolerant species, it is also adaptable to a wide range of soil types and frost-tolerant to at least −8°C.

H: 25 m tree	Frost-hardy
20 cm prostrate shrub	Attracts birds
F: Autumn–spring	

Banksia media

Southern plains banksia, golden stalk

This species forms a rounded, bushy shrub to usually less than 3 m under cultivation, although occasionally it may become a tree of 10 m. A prostrate form has excellent garden potential but is not yet generally available.

The handsome, squat, cylindrical flower heads of golden yellow are usually about 15 cm long and can be produced both on short stems from old wood and terminally on outer branches. They are carried from autumn through winter into spring.

Banksia integrifolia produces massed displays of these yellow-green cones for months on end, to the delight of nectar-seeking birds.

One of the easier West Australian species to grow outside its natural habitat, *B. media* will grow in most well-drained soil types, including slightly alkaline ones. It is tolerant of salt spray, midwinter frost to –5°C and may be grown in both full sun and partial shade.

H: 3 m shrub	Medium frost-hardy
10 m tree	Attracts birds
F: Autumn–spring	Cut flowers

Not always an easy subject in cultivation, *B. menziesii* requires very free-draining, lighter soils and sunny positions, but will tolerate light frost and salt winds. With its free-flowering habit it is certainly one of the most attractive banksia species for the garden.

H: 2 m	Attracts birds
F: Autumn–winter	Cut flowers
Tolerates light frosts	

Banksia media is one of the easier Western Australia species to grow in the garden.

Banksia menziesii

Menzies' banksia, firewood banksia, 'Raspberry Frost'

In nature this West Australian species can become a gnarled tree of up to 15 m, but the more desirable selected compact forms under cultivation rarely exceed 1.5–2 m. Becauses it responds well to hard pruning, it is easy to keep to a manageable size. A gorgeous cut flower (it is marketed as 'Raspberry Frost' by growers in Hawaii) the large, acorn-shaped, multi-coloured heads are produced over autumn and winter on long stems. Commencing as long buds of an appealing silver-grey colour, they become red with silver-toned vertical rows as they develop, with the golden flowers opening from the base to create a symmetrical sculpture.

Banksia menziesii, with its delightful colour combinations, is a popular cut flower on world markets.

Banksia nutans

Nodding banksia

Although this novel species from the southern coast of Western Australia is little known in cultivation, from time to time specialist nurseries list it, and the nodding banksia is worthy of a position in the connoisseur's garden. A neat, bushy shrub to around 1 m in height, *B. nutans* has heath-like blue-green foliage. The very distinctive pinkish-purple nodding pendant flower heads that are produced from spring right through summer into autumn are often onion-scented. The old seed cones persist on the shrub for some years.

This species is considered unreliable in warm, humid climates but is easily grown in cooler, dry climates. Grafting onto *B. ericifolia* rootstock has increased the cultivation range. It is frost-hardy to at least –3°C, can be grown in either full sun or semi-shade, and requires well-drained, lighter soils. Light pruning within green foliage can encourage compact growth habits.

H: 1 m	Medium frost-hardy
F: Spring–autumn	

The nodding banksia has unusual pendant flower heads of pinkish purple, big seed cones and fine foliage.

Banksia occidentalis

Red swamp banksia, waterbush, 'Indian Summer'

Under cultivation this species is generally a bushy shrub some 3 m high with an almost equal spread, although in its natural habitat of southern Western Australia it may become a small tree of 7 m. This desirable garden plant is attractive to nectar-seeking birds, is wind-tolerant and can withstand damp soils to a greater extent than many proteaceous plants. It will survive frost to about –4°C.

Banksia occidentalis is noted for tolerating moist soils.

Foliage is long (to 12 cm) and narrow (to 3 mm), bright green on the upper surface and silver-grey on the undersides. The flower spikes are an appealing glossy red colour, cylindrically shaped to 14 cm long and mainly produced during the summer and autumn months. These are used as cut flowers by commercial growers, particularly in Hawaii.

Although commonly known as swamp banksia, *B. occidentalis* should not be grown in excessively wet soils, but it will benefit from watering in dry periods.

H: 7 m tree	Medium frost-hardy
3 m shrub	Attracts birds
F: Summer–autumn	Cut flowers

Banksia ornata

Desert banksia, saw-leaved scrub honeysuckle

This species originates from south-west Victoria and south-east South Australia. A bushy shrub, 2.5–3 m high, *B. ornata* has cylindrical flower spikes up to 14 cm in length, which vary in colour from greyish yellow to golden bronze and are mainly produced over winter and spring. Because this species is noted for having pollen particularly high in protein, it is well regarded by beekeepers. Large quantities of nectar are also produced, making the flowers attractive to birds.

The desert banksia grows well in sandy and other well-drained soils. Drought-tolerant once established, it is happiest in open, sunny positions and will withstand light frost. It can also be successfully grown as a large tub plant for a time but will eventually need to be transferred to the open ground.

H: 3 m	Tolerates light frosts
F: Winter–spring	Attracts birds

Banksia ornata is suitable for growing in a large tub.

Banksia praemorsa

Cut-leaf banksia

A particularly attractive species, the cut-leaf banksia has distinctive small (rarely more than 40 mm long) bright green leaves with sharply cut-off tips. The large flower spikes are cylindrical, up to 30 cm long and 10 cm in diameter. The colouring is hard to define, being a blend of many tones with an overall deep fawn appearance. They are initially a reddish maroon and at maturity become a golden shade, with the deep fawn an intermediate stage. Blooms are produced freely from late winter through spring to early summer, depending to some extent on the locality in which they are being cultivated. Growth habit is dense and a height of up to 4 m may be attained. It is regarded both as an attractive specimen shrub that withstands some light pruning and shaping, and a useful screening subject.

While *B. praemorsa* requires very well-drained soils, it is best suited to areas of predominantly winter rainfall. Warm humid climates are unlikely to be conducive to successful cultivation of this West Australian banksia. It is surprisingly resistant to salt spray and is often grown to perfection in sandy seaside gardens. It can withstand frosts to about –3°C.

H: 4 m	Tolerates light frosts
F: Winter–summer	Attracts birds

Banksia praemorsa produces very large heads of bloom that change colour as they develop.

Banksia 'Waite Orange', a *B. hookeriana* x *B. prionotes* selection developed by the University of Adelaide. The large flower spikes are very similar to those of the *B. prionotes* parent but are produced more prolifically.

Banksia prionotes

Acorn banksia, orange banksia, golden banksia, 'Orange Frost'

This spectacular species produces particularly large acorn-shaped flower spikes of rich orange during autumn and winter. These may be 15 cm or more in length and are carried on long stems. It is grown commercially as a cut flower in Australia, Hawaii and Israel. The mature bush may vary in height from a spreading bush of 3 m to a small tree of 10 m and has particularly long (to 30 cm) leaves, which are regularly toothed, grey-green in colour and often have a waved or undulating appearance. Under cultivation a regular light pruning is necessary to maintain a tidy habit.

As with most of the West Australian species, this banksia requires very well-drained soils that are not excessively high in nutrient levels. Occasional frosts to –4°C are tolerated.

H: 3 m shrub	Medium frost-hardy
10 m tree	Attracts birds
F: Autumn–winter	Cut flowers

Banksia robur

Swamp banksia, broad-leaved banksia

This distinctive banksia bears very large, leathery leaves to 30 cm long and 10 cm wide. They have waved margins that are lightly serrated. and the young growth is velvety and rusty brown in appearance. Flowers are a deep blue-green at the bud stage before opening to a greenish-yellow colour. They are produced over summer through to winter and can be up to 15 cm long. Although usually terminal (at the ends of the stems), these flower spikes may also be found in clusters on lower stems. They are attractive to both birds and bees.

While generally an open shrub of some 2 m height, this species has a lignotuber, which enables it to shoot into vigorous new growth after hard pruning. This ability is beneficial in the garden situation, where a more compact plant may be desired. The swamp banksia is adaptable to varying soils, including heavy, slow-draining types. It is also easily grown in both cool and warm climates.

H: 2 m	Medium frost-hardy
F: Summer–winter	Attracts birds

LEFT: The flower spikes of *Banksia robur* are a metallic blue-green at the bud stage.

RIGHT: The velvety, rust-coloured young growth is a feature.

Banksia serrata

Saw banksia, red honeysuckle, red banksia, old man banksia

This is the banksia of Australian children's books where reference is made to 'Old Man Banksia' or the 'Big Bad Banksia Men', alluding to the large, knobbly seed cones that are so prominent on older, gnarled examples of this small tree. An excellent 'character tree' for landscaping purposes, *B. serrata* produces conspicuous, broadly cylindrical flower spikes that can be 15 cm long and 12 cm wide when fully developed. These are a yellowish-green colour, borne from midsummer into winter and are attractive to nectar-seeking birds. Not

RIGHT: *Banksia serrata*, old man banksia, has spectacular flower heads.

normally used for commercial picking, owing to short stems, they do, however, have an excellent vase life. The bright green leaves are tough, strongly serrated and up to 15 cm long. Old bushes may be up to 15 m high and of open habit in nature, but it is more usual to see cultivated specimens that are densely branched and 3–4 m in height. *B. serrata* withstands quite hard pruning to keep it to manageable proportions.

The 'red' in some of the common names refers to the colour of the oak-like timber, which has been used for various purposes including boat building.

Native to Tasmania and the east coast of Australia into Queensland, this long-lived species is easily grown in many parts of the world. It thrives in most well-drained soils, is frost-hardy and will tolerate salt-laden winds. A semi-prostrate form, reaching to no more than 60 cm high with a spread of 2.5 m or more, has been marketed in Australia under the name of 'Austraflora Pygmy Possum' and is noted for its suitability for coastal gardens.

H: 4–15 m	Frost-hardy
F: Summer–winter	Attracts birds

Banksia speciosa

Showy banksia, rickrack banksia, green banksia, 'Mint Julep'

The squatly cylindrical, almost acorn-shaped, large flower spikes of this banksia are a silver-grey colour at the bud stage, but then become a bright lemon or chartreuse shade as they open. Carried terminally on long, sturdy stems over summer and autumn, these blooms are grown as commercial cut flowers in several parts of the world, notably Hawaii. Foliage is long (45 cm), narrow, wavy and deeply serrated, and is very characteristic of this species. Native to the southern coast of Western Australia, *B. speciosa* reaches to 5 m in height with a greater spread, and is used to good effect as a windbreak or screen plant as well as for picking.

Light, very well-drained soils are a prerequisite to successful cultivation of this species, which thrives in sandy conditions near the coast. It survives salt winds and is frost-tolerant to –3°C.

H: 3–10 m	Attracts birds
F: Autumn–winter	Cut flowers
Medium frost-hardy	

Banksia spinulosa

Hairpin banksia

This is generally a compact shrub that rarely exceeds 2 m in height and occurs naturally throughout eastern Australia, from southern Victoria through New South Wales to most of coastal Queensland in varying forms. Some forms are taller, to 6 m, but these tend to be less popular in cultivation. The large cylindrical flower cones can measure 18 cm long and 8 cm in diameter, are produced over autumn and winter, and are attractive to birds. Colour is variable, ranging from soft gold through to orange-red shadings. The hooked black

Banksia speciosa is a versatile shrub well suited to coastal conditions.

styles are very characteristic. Leaves are narrow, up to 12 cm long, and have short teeth that are more pronounced towards the tips.

There are varying forms under cultivation, some of more dwarf habit, and the species previously known as *B. collina* has now been classified as a variety of *B. spinulosa*. A popular, 'Austraflora Birthday Candles', has dense foliage and neat, erectly held flower cones of soft golden yellow over winter. It has a dense, spreading habit to 1.5 m wide and 30 cm high, and has proved successful in rockeries and planters and as a spectacular tub plant for patios and similar situations.

An easy plant to cultivate, this banksia will thrive in most well-drained soils in sunny positions and is one of the more frost-hardy species. It will tolerate hard pruning and can therefore be controlled easily in the garden situation.

H: Variable	Frost-hardy
F: Autumn–winter	Attracts birds

Banksia spinulosa 'Austraflora Birthday Candles', usually known as simply 'Birthday Candles', is a stunning tub plant as well as being superb in rock gardens and planters.

CONOSPERMUM

This genus of some 36 species is distributed throughout much of coastal eastern Australia, south-west Western Australia, South Australia and Tasmania. The West Australian species in particular have been widely exploited for cut-flower purposes.

Conospermum mitchellii

Grampians smoke-bush, Victorian smoke-bush, mountain conospermum

In nature this species occurs in a restricted area of western Victoria in Australia; mainly in the Grampians and the Otway Ranges and just over the border into South Australia. Usually a bushy or semi-erect shrub of some 2 m with a lesser spread, it needs to be pruned after flowering each year to maintain a compact growth habit. It is a useful background shrub and may have some commercial potential for picking purposes.

The small white or smoky-grey flowers are borne in dense terminal corymbs up to 15 cm wide during spring and early summer. These are sometimes picked for floral work, being useful filler material, and may also be dried.

Banksia spinulosa, commonly known as the hairpin banksia.

The Grampians smokebush is often used in floral
arrangements.

Adaptable to most well-drained soils, this species is
drought-tolerant once established and may be grown
in either full sun or filtered shade. It is tolerant of light
frost to –3°C.

H: 2 m	Light–medium frost-hardy
F: Spring– early summer	Cut flowers

DARLINGIA

There are just two recorded species of this tropical rainforest genus from northern Queensland in Australia.
Both have particularly handsome foliage and beautiful
sprays of cream flowers. Neither is widely cultivated at
present, but darlingas are becoming more readily available to gardeners in warm climates.

Darlingia ferruginea

Rose silky oak, silky oak, brown silky oak

This particularly beautiful tree is from the Atherton and
Evelyn Tablelands area of Australia's northern Queensland. While it may reach to 30 m in height in its dense
rainforest habitat, it is more usual to see it as a slender
tree of 10 m or less under cultivation.

The very large leaves are deeply lobed, 60–70 cm long,
with prominent veins, and the undersides are coated
with rust-coloured hairs that are also noticeable on
young stems. The specific name indicates a rusty-red
colour.

The prominent creamy-white flowers are borne in
long racemes and are similar to those of *Macadamia*.
They are produced during winter and early spring, and
have an attractive scent.

Both species of *Darlingia* have been logged for their
attractively grained reddish-brown timber, which has
been used for cabinet work. They make spectacular,
fast-growing specimen trees for larger gardens and,
while young, are handsome indoor plants.

This frost-tender genus requires rich, moisture-
retentive but free-draining loamy soils and warm, sunny
positions.

Darlingia may be propagated from both seed and
cuttings.

H: 10 m	Frost-tender
F: Winter– early spring	

Darlingia ferruginea, seen here in bud, is a beautiful
Queensland rainforest member of the Protea family.

DRYANDRA

Named after Jonas Dryander, a Swedish botanist who served as librarian to Sir Joseph Banks and also the original librarian at the Linnean Society of London, the genus *Dryandra* has 57 species, with more to be added as they are described. They occur naturally only in the south-west area of Western Australia and range from prostrate species, known as honeypots because of the large amounts of nectar they produce, through bushy shrubs to erect examples of 3 m or more in height.

Foliage is amazingly variable, some species having very narrow leaves with small, jagged margins, others with a coarse, fishbone appearance, and still others have large leaves like a banksia.

Flowers also are likely to be quite different from one species to the next. Some may be like open tufted shaving brushes, while others may be more closed, with distinct outer bracts resembling a small protea flower head. Colours are usually restricted to the bronze and yellow tonings.

This fascinating genus deserves wider acceptance by gardeners, especially those having well-drained light soils, mild climates and sunny, dry positions. Some species produce excellent cut flowers for long-lasting arrangements; others make superb rockery subjects with their low-growing, neat habits and intriguing foliage and flower combinations.

Unfortunately, very few *Dryandra* species are in general cultivation and, accordingly, just two of the more readily obtainable ones are discussed below.

Dryandra formosa

Showy dryandra, golden emperor

The aptly named showy dryandra comes from the southern region of Western Australia, in particular the Stirling Range, where it is found at all altitudes. Usually a tall shrub of dense habit and up to 3.5 m high, it may sometimes be more open when grown in harsh conditions. Under cultivation in good conditions it can assume an almost pyramidal shape of 2.5 m.

The dark-green leaves are up to 120 mm long, narrow and deeply cut, almost to the midrib. They have a saw-like appearance.

The terminal flower heads are held conspicuously above the foliage and may often be clustered in tight masses of flowers and buds. They are a rich bronze prior to opening to a golden-orange shade. Up to 8 cm wide,

Dryandra formosa is the most widely cultivated member of the genus.

blooms are borne over most of the year, with a peak during spring. This is a striking ornamental shrub for the home garden but also is grown in several parts of the world as a cut flower, with an excellent vase life, and is also able to be dried. Nectar-seeking birds are attracted to the flowers

One of the hardiest species of the genus (and easily propagated from seed), *D. formosa* prefers a light, free-draining soil and a sunny position. It tends to be shallow-rooted so may need some protection from high winds, but will tolerate frost to –5°C.

H: 2.5–3.5 m	Medium frost-tender
F: Year-round,	Attracts birds
especially spring	Cut flowers

Dryandra nivea

Couch honeypot

The best known of the prostrate honeypot species (though by no means the most spectacular), *D. nivea* can also develop into a cushion-like bush 40 cm high.

The densely packed foliage, especially where it surrounds the flowers, may be up to 30 cm long. Deep green, often with white undersides, the leaves have deeply toothed and regular margins.

The low-growing *Dryandra nivea* is well suited to rock gardens and planters.

The flowers, which resemble shaving brushes, are usually orange-bronze in colour (sometimes white) and are carried over winter and spring. Borne deep within the foliage, they are sometimes almost hidden.

Native to the south-west of Western Australia, this is an excellent rockery plant It enjoys full sun or semi-shade, is adaptable to a wide range of soil types and is quite hardy, standing up to frosts as hard as −7°C once established. *D. nivea* is usually propagated by seed.

H: 30–40 cm	Frost-hardy
F: Winter–spring	

EMBOTHRIUM

This small genus of trees and shrubs is mainly confined to the Andes Mountains in Chile. It originally included the species that have now been split into *Oreocallis*, *Alloxylon*, *Telopea*, *Stenocarpus* and *Lomatia*. The best-known species is described here.

Embothrium coccineum

Chilean fire bush

This is generally an erect, slender tree of up to 6 m in height, but under cultivation will often sucker and form thickets of dense growth if uncontrolled. A well-grown example may have branches weeping to the ground with the weight of the abundant spring flowers. These are carried in dense clusters, are honeysuckle-like, a rich orange-red in colour and so prolific that the common name is particularly appropriate. While spring is the main flowering time, some blooms can occur over summer and autumn.

Foliage is lanceolate, deep green, up to 14 cm long and variable in width from 2 to 3 cm. The cultivar 'lanceolatum' has narrower leaves, is regarded as being more frost-hardy and can become semi-deciduous in cold climates. *Embothrium coccineum* is a well-known garden subject in many parts of the world, including Australia, New Zealand, California and milder areas in the United Kingdom. A particularly colourful small tree, it may be used as a specimen tree or as background to shrub borders.

Soils that are free-draining yet moisture-retentive because of adequate organic material are necessary. High rainfall is common in the Andes habitat, so *Embothrium* benefits from an occasional deep watering during dry summer conditions.

Narrow-leaved cultivars such as 'lanceolatum' are reputed to be more tolerant of hard pruning than the broader-leaved types, which may not shoot back into growth as readily.

H: 6 m	Frost-hardy
F: Spring-summer	Attracts birds

The Chilean fire bush, *Embothrium coccineum*, is a colourful choice for colder climates.

GEVUINA

This South American member of the Proteaceae is rapidly gaining attention as a valuable nut crop. It has been likened to a cool-climate macadamia and intensive work is being undertaken at research institutes to select the best forms for commercial purposes.

Gevuina avellana

Chilean hazelnut, avellano, guevin, neufén

An ornamental medium-sized tree, native to southern Chile and Argentina, this is the southern-most species in the Macadamieae tribe of the Proteaceae.

Gevuina allevana reaches about 12 m high with a compact canopy of large leathery bipinnate leaves divided into glossy dark green leaflets that are lightly serrated. Young growth is covered in reddish-brown hair. Foliage is used for garnishing food and also by florists. The handsomely grained timber is sometimes used in turning and for musical instruments.

Creamy-white macadamia-like flowers are borne in spectacular clusters that show up well against the dark-green foliage. These are produced during late summer and have copious amounts of nectar to attract bees and other pollinators. The green fruit turn to bright red before becoming brown or black at the fully developed nut stage. As they take almost twelve months to mature, the nuts can be seen on the tree at the same time as the flowers of the following season. A tree with both red fruit and white flowers set against the attractive foliage is a delightful sight, whether in a home garden or commercial orchard.

Unlike the very hard macadamia, gevuina nuts have a soft husk that is easily peeled with a knife. They are generally slightly smaller than macadamia, although some cultivars being selected are of a similar size. They have high levels of oils useful for cosmetic purposes and table oil, are rich in protein, have less fat than macadamia and are considered to have excellent prospects as a health food.

Frost-hardy to −8°C, suitable for most good, well-drained soils, adaptable to either full sun or partial shade, *Gevuina* will require shelter from high wind and, because it has proteoid roots, fertilisers high in phosphate should be avoided.

H: 12 m	Frost-hardy
F: Late summer	Useful foliage

Gevuina avellana has highly ornamental foliage and attractive, macadamia-like flower racemes. The fruit develop into high-quality nuts.

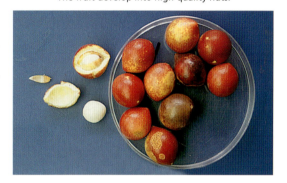

GREVILLEA

The Australian genus of *Grevillea* comprises about 273 species, 61 subspecies and, at the time of writing, about 200 cultivars, a number that is increasing continually. Several books have been produced solely on this genus, indicating the interest that exists in grevilleas as well as the complexity of the subject.

Named for Charles Francis Greville, who was one of the founders of the Royal Horticultural Society in 1804, this genus of the Proteaceae has become cultivated by gardeners in many parts of the world. Hardier species and cultivars have been grown in parts of the United Kingdom for more than 100 years, and there are about 100 species and cultivars reported to be available in the United States. Grevilleas are also widely grown in South Africa and the Riviera, while the tropical species are also cultivated in warmer parts of South-east Asia.

This is an amazingly variable genus, with growth habits ranging from the prostrate, groundcover types through dense shrubs to tall trees. Flowers not only range in colour from white through pink, orange and

Tropical grevillea flowers make an eye-catching arrangement.

yellow to red, but may be small and spider-like or large, toothbrush-shaped and flamboyantly coloured. Foliage can be sharp and needle-like or resembling big, soft fern leaves. Some species are very hardy, while others will burn at the slightest hint of frost.

Within the restrictions imposed by the broad coverage of this book, a representative range of grevilleas is offered in attempt to convey the fascination and complexity of the genus and to encourage more gardeners to cultivate these plants.

Grevillea 'Aussie Crawl'

This relatively recent introduction is typical of the many outstanding hybrid groundcover grevilleas that are being brought into cultivation by enterprising nurseries in Australia. A similar hybrid is 'Fanfare'.

The attractive, 10 cm long, lobed foliage of 'Aussie Crawler' is a deep green colour, with the underside a lighter, almost lustrous silvery green. New growth is pale bronze. Rich red toothbrush-type flowers are produced in abundance from winter through the spring months into early summer.

A vigorous and spreading habit, to around 3 m wide, makes this grevillea valuable for covering a variety of situations, from disguising difficult banks to helping

Grevillea 'Aussie Crawl' is one of several newer, outstanding groundcover cultivars.

eliminate weeds in flat garden situations, and training to spill over walls. Regular pruning will encourage thicker growth.

As with most of this type of groundcover grevillea, 'Aussie Crawl' is hardy, withstanding frosts, dry, windy situations and poor soils. It is equally at home in warmer, humid environs. Being a hybrid, this grevillea must be propagated from cuttings to ensure progeny is replicated.

| H: 10–15 cm x 3 m wide | Frost-hardy |
| F: Winter–early summer | Attracts birds |

Grevillea baileyana

White oak, Findlay's silky oak

An intriguing tropical species from Northern Queensland in Australia's tropical region, *G. baileyana* is being increasingly grown as a garden and landscaping subject. It is more cold-hardy than one would suppose, and is cultivated as far south as Coffs Harbour in New South Wales. While it may reach a height of 25 m in its warm rainforest habitat, it is rare to see it exceeding 8 or 10 m under cultivation, where it branches to form a dense, large shrub. In nature it is sometimes logged at maturity for its pink-toned timber.

The foliage is handsome, being a glossy deep green on the upper surface while the undersides are covered in a mass of fine, silky, golden-brown or silvery hairs. It is variable in leaf form at the juvenile stage, often being deeply lobed, but at the mature stage it is entire and may be 20 cm long. This attractive foliage provides a foil for the massed panicles of creamy-white bloom produced over spring and summer.

This grevillea is sometimes used as an indoor plant in cooler climates and is a fast-growing and very ornamental subject for tropical gardens. Good soil, a frost-free situation and sun or partial shade are the preferred conditions.

| H: 8–25 m | Frost-tender |
| F: Spring–summer | |

Grevillea baileyana, a spectacular tropical Australia species, is popular in Queensland gardens.

Grevillea banksii

(syn. *G. banksii* var. *forsteri*)

Banks' grevillea, red-flowered silky oak, red silky oak

This grevillea is so variable that it can be difficult to describe accurately. The form most widespread and common in its native coastal Queensland flowers for a brief period in spring, whereas the form commonly grown in gardens flowers year round and is often marketed as *G. banksii* var. *fosteri* or 'Foster's'. Generally the spectacularly large (10 cm long) flowers are a pinkish-red colour, but both cream- and red-flowered prostrate forms are also grown.

This is an important grevillea species, being one of the parents of many outstanding hybrids, 'Robyn Gordon', 'Superb', 'Coconut Ice' and 'Misty Pink' being just a few examples. It is frequently hybridised with *G. bipinnatifida*.

The usual, cultivated form of *G. banksii* grows up to 4 m but is more often seen as a well-shaped and pruned shrub of 2–3 m with an equal spread. The prostrate red and cream forms are very distinctive and are sometimes grafted onto *G. robusta* rootstock to form spectacular standards.

This subtropical species will tolerate the occasional very light frost but is seen at its best in warm climates.

It is widely grown in several areas of the world, including parts of New Zealand, warm regions of the United States and in South-east Asia. *G. banksii* is tolerant of salt spray so is frequently used to spectacular effect in coastal gardens. It has the added bonus of being especially attractive to nectar-seeking birds.

H: 2–3 m	Frost-tender
(also prostrate forms)	Attracts birds
F: Year-round	
(white form, spring)	

Grevillea barklyana

Gully grevillea, large-leaf grevillea

This vigorous shrub or small tree reaches a maximum height of 8 m in southern Victoria, but 3 m is more usual under cultivation. There is also a subspecies, *G. barklyana* subsp. *macleayana*, which is lower-growing, has oval leaves and is more suitable for warmer climates.

The usual species has attractive foliage, the large, deep green leaves being silvery on the undersides, while young growth is a bronze colour. The deep pink toothbrush-like flowers, which are attractive to birds, are

ABOVE: The red-flowered prostrate form of *Grevillea banksii* can be used as a groundcover or, grafted, as a standard weeper.

BELOW: The less common cream-flowered prostrate form of *G. banksii* has much potential.

Grevillea barklyana is a fast-growing species well suited to screening purposes.

ABOVE and RIGHT: The flowers and foliage of *G. barklyana* are used for floral arrangements.

prominently displayed over late winter and spring.

G. barklyana is equally at home in sun or partial shade, but is damaged by strong winds, being quite shallow-rooted and with branches that break easily. However, it makes an excellent screening subject and is also used for cut foliage for florists' backing material. It is easily propagated from semi-hardwood cuttings.

H: 3 m shrub	Frost-hardy
8 m tree	Attracts birds
F: Late winter–spring	Cut foliage

Grevillea 'Bon Accord'

(syn. *G.* 'Australflora Bon Accord')

The original name of this outstanding cultivar, 'Australflora Bon Accord', reflects the name of the originating nursery in Victoria and commemorates a summit meeting between US and USSR leaders.

This grevillea is a hybrid between *G. johnsonii* (from the south of Western Australia) and *G. wilsonii* (New South Wales) and forms a densely erect bush of 2 x 2 m. It has deeply divided foliage with bronze new growth and brilliant red flowers, which are carried in dense terminal clusters from late winter through spring to summer, and are attractive to birds.

'Bon Accord' is equally adaptable to average, well-drained soils and dry conditions. It will thrive in both full sun and partial shade, and is tolerant of light to medium frost.

The example at right was photographed in late winter at Fairhill Native Plant Nursery and Gardens in Yandina, Queensland.

H: 2 m	Medium frost-hardy
F: Late winter–summer	Attracts birds

Grevillea 'Australflora Bon Accord' is a brilliantly coloured versatile cultivar.

'Boongala Spinebill' – an intriguing name and a hardy, attractive grevillea for the garden.

'Bronze Rambler' proves its value as a handsome plant for softening landscape features as it cascades down this timber retaining wall.

Grevillea 'Boongala Spinebill'

Another hybrid (supposedly *G. bipinnatifida* x *G. caleyi*) with Western Australia and New South Wales parentage, this cultivar carries the name 'Boongala' to identify the property where it originated, while 'Spinebill' refers to a group of honey-eating birds.

This attractive bushy shrub of 2 m in height tends to have a semi-weeping habit, with foliage often reaching the ground. The narrow, very divided leaves are slightly prickly and are a deep glossy green. Young growth is a light reddish-brown shade. The prominent deep crimson toothbrush flowers are produced year-round, are pendulous and sought after by nectar-seeking birds.

This very adaptable cultivar tolerates frost, drought and humidity – an unusual combination. It is regarded as one of the hardiest of the landscape grevilleas and can be used as a specimen, in mixed borders or for screening purposes.

G. 'Boongala Spinebill' responds well to regular pruning and can be shaped accordingly. Good drainage appears to be the only requirement for its successful cultivation.

H: 2 m	Frost-hardy
F: Year-round	Attracts birds

Grevillea 'Bronze Rambler'

The new growth of this appropriately named cultivar is distinctly bronze-coloured and the plant's habit is very rambling, generally to no more than 30 cm high but up to 4 m or so wide. The dark green leaves are narrowly and deeply lobed, and very characteristic of this grevillea. A very dense intertwining of foliage and branchlets creates a tough, impenetrable net-like mass, with pinkish-red toothbrush flowers well displayed for much of the year, but especially during spring and early summer.

This is hardy and adaptable grevillea has multiple applications in the garden. A maintenance-free groundcover, it can also be used to disguise a difficult bank or soften a high wall. Grafted onto rootstocks of *G. robusta*, it will form an attractive weeping standard.

Frost-hardy and adaptable to sun or shade, humid conditions and a range of soil conditions, *G.* 'Bronze Rambler' seems to thrive in almost any well-drained garden, regardless of climate.

H: 30 cm x 4 m wide	Frost-hardy
F: Year-round	Attracts birds

Both flowers and foliage are features of the vigorous *Grevillea* 'Bronze Rambler'.

Grevillea 'Canberra Gem'

(syn. *G.* 'Pink Pearl', *G.* 'Canberra')

'Canberra Gem' is the result of an intentional cross, or manipulation, between *G. juniperina* and *G. rosmarinifolia*. One of the earliest of such cultivars, dating to the early 1960s and significant for this alone, it is also an excellent choice for a dense, formal hedge, responding well to regular clipping, and can become an almost impenetrable boundary for keeping unwanted animals out of the garden. The normal growth habit is that of a dense shrub of 2.5 x 2.5 m.

The small, narrow, deep green pointed leaves are about 30 mm long and provide an excellent foil for the large clusters of waxy pink 'spider' flowers that are borne year-round but are especially prominent during winter and spring. They have the added benefit of being attractive to nectar-seeking birds.

'Canberra Gem' is a particularly hardy and easily grown grevillea that can be seen in gardens as far from its origins as England and parts of the United States. Tolerant of heavy frost once established, it will grow in almost any well-drained soil but can be more difficult to grow in hot, humid climates.

Photograph on page 64.

H: 2.5 m	Frost-hardy
F: Year-round	Attracts birds

Grevillea 'Coconut Ice'

This cultivar is a further example of the almost never-ending range of hybrids to be produced from *G. banksii* x *G. bipinnatifida* manipulation. In this instance the white-flowered form of *G. banksii* was reputedly used as the male parent. The foliage is typically large and softly pinnate, and similar to that of 'Robyn Gordon'. It is larger growing, however, reaching to 2 m high with a similar spread. Regular pruning is desirable and hard cutting back encourages vigorous new growth.

The large racemes of flowers, to at least 15 cm long, are more open in appearance than those of 'Robyn Gordon'. A soft pinkish red with deep red-coloured styles, they are produced throughout the year, to the delight of nectar-seeking birds.

As with most of the *G. banksii* cultivars, warm, sheltered positions in the garden are preferred. Good drainage and either a sunny or partial-shade position are desirable.

H: 2 m	Frost-tender
F: Year-round	Attracts birds

Grevillea 'Coconut Ice' is one of many spectacular hybrids resulting from *G. banksii* x *G. bipinnatifida* manipulation.

Grevillea depauperata

(Previously *G. brownii* – prostrate form)

'Orange Glow' is a selected form of *G. depauperata* that retains its prostrate growth habit, making it a particularly useful plant for overhanging banks and walls. More usually a small, dense shrub of up to 1 m, this attractive groundcover form reaches less than 30 cm high, with a spread of a metre or more. Being less vigorous than many other grevillea groundcovers, it is an ideal subject for smaller gardens and as a container plant. The small oval deep-green leaves are little more than 20 mm long and provide a striking contrast with the brilliant red 'spider' flowers borne in terminal clusters from autumn through winter and into spring. These attract nectar-seeking birds.

This grevillea tolerates frosts to –5°C and can be grown in either sun or semi-shade, but must have well-drained soil to prevent root disease. In its ideal planting position of hanging over banks and walls or spilling over rockeries, drainage is unlikely to pose a problem.

H: 1 m	Medium frost-hardy
F: Autumn–spring	Attracts birds

LEFT: 'Canberra Gem' is a very hardy cultivar that is used for a variety of landscape purposes.

BELOW: *Grevillea depauperata* cv. 'Orange Glow' forms a delightful curtain of red bloom over an old concrete wall.

Grevillea dryandri is a spectacular species for warm-climate gardens.

Grevillea dryandri

Dryander oak, Maytown grevillea

Although rarely seen in gardens outside Australia, this unusual species is noteworthy for its large flower racemes, which can be up to 30 cm long. Usually seen in bright red or pink tones, they may also occur in white or cream. The much-divided, 20 cm long grey-green leaves have an almost fish-skeleton appearance, adding to the charm of this species.

Growth habit is generally low and spreading, usually less than 70 cm high with a spread of of up to 2 m. It is sometimes grafted onto a standard to give a handsome and unusual weeping specimen. There is also a subspecies with a taller growth habit.

G. dryandri is regarded as a desirable smaller species for warm-climate gardens, with a spectacular display of large blooms that attract birds. Sun and good drainage are vital to successful cultivation: this is an ideal rockery subject. Though native to tropical regions of Australia, it will survive light frosts.

| H: 70 cm | Tolerates light frosts |
| F: Autumn-winter | Attracts birds |

'Elegance' has delightful bicoloured flowers.

Grevillea 'Elegance'

(syn. G. 'Poorinda Elegance')

The nursery trade and gardening public seem to have gradually abbreviated the full names of 'Poorinda' and 'Australflora' grevillea cultivars. 'Poorinda Elegance', usually called simply 'Elegance', is a hybrid between G. juniperina and another hybrid, G. obtusiflora x G. alpina. It is a vigorous shrub to 2 x 2m with small, glossy, blunt foliage that responds well to pruning.

Flowers are unusual and bicoloured, being soft apricot with a conspicuous red style, and are produced continually from spring through summer into autumn. Unfortunately, they are found on the older wood, but a light pruning of new growth in early spring will allow the blooms to be well displayed.

This easily grown cultivar is frost-hardy and adaptable to a wide range of well-drained soil types in either full sun or semi-shade. It makes an excellent hedge or screen plant.

| H: 2 m | Frost-hardy |
| F: Spring–autumn | Attracts birds |

Grevillea 'Fanfare'

(syn. G. 'Australflora Fanfare')

This very vigorous groundcover cultivar should be popular with gardeners and local authority organisations seeking to cover large areas of ground, thus suppressing weeds while providing visual appeal. A chance seedling believed to be a hybrid between G. x gaudichaudii and G. longifolia originating in a garden in the state of Victoria, this grevillea can spread to a width of some 5 m with a virtually flat habit. Tip pruning will encourage the much-branched habit.

Leaves are noticeably deeper and more regular than some similar cultivars and have copper-coloured young growth. The typical toothbrush flowers are a rich winered colour and carried over spring, summer and autumn.

As with most similar groundcover grevilleas, 'Fanfare' thrives in temperate climates; humid subtropical areas often promote fungal problems and subsequent defoliation and spotting. A hardy hybrid, it tolerates both frost and drought. This –grevillea has potential for grafting onto standard rootstocks to create attractive weeping specimens.

| H: 30 cm | Frost-hardy |
| F: Spring–autumn | Attracts birds |

RIGHT: Grevillea 'Fanfare' is a vigorous and hardy groundcover.

Grevillea fasciculata

This grevillea is variable in form, ranging from an upright shrub of 1 m to low, spreading variations. The prostrate form has proved most popular with gardeners. This will become a dense shrub of little more than 30 cm high but with a spread of 1.5 m in good conditions. While superficially similar to *G. depauperata* 'Orange Glow', it has smaller, lighter-coloured flowers. The leaves, too, are smaller and a lighter green.

The foliage is dark green with a light grey underside and is tightly massed, thus providing good groundcover.

The small spider flowers are a bright scarlet-red and carried in tight little racemes or clusters at the ends of the branches from winter through spring.

While regarded as hardy in its native Western Australia, it can be damaged by frosts of –5°C. A delightful and very colourful groundcover, *G. fasciculata* is also well suited to both rockery and wall-hanging applications. It has also been successfully grown in tubs. Good drainage, sun and an open position with good air circulation are required for successful cultivation.

H: 30 cm x 1.5 m wide   Medium frost-hardy
F: Winter–spring

Grevillea fasciculata cascades over rocks, creating a river of orange-scarlet bloom over winter and spring.

Grevillea formosa

Mount Brockman grevillea

The specific name comes from the Latin *formosus*, meaning beautiful. This magnificent grevillea from the north of Australia's Northern Territory can usually be grown successfully by gardeners fortunate to live in warm, frost-free climates. Forming a low, spreading bush of 70 cm high by 2.5 m across, *G. formosa* is sometimes used as a tall groundcover. It has also been grafted onto taller rootstocks to create a weeping specimen.

Grevillea formosa is a beautiful low-growing shrub for frost-free climates. It is also used as a weeping standard in tubs.

The foliage alone is reason enough to cultivate this species, the finely divided silvery-grey leaves being up to 18 cm long and quite spectacular.

The huge flower racemes can measure 30 cm long and are equally handsome at the lime-green bud stage in spring or the golden-yellow flower stage over summer and autumn.

H: 70 cm   Frost-tender
F: Summer–autumn

Grevillea x gaudichaudii

Grevillea x *gaudichaudii* is a naturally occurring hybrid between *G. laurifolia* and *G. acanthifolia* and is seen in nature in the Blue Mountains area of New South Wales. It has been in cultivation for a number of years and is well established as an excellent groundcover for cool-climate gardens. Growth habit of this grevillea is prostrate, reaching no more than 15 cm high, but spreading

A popular groundcover grevillea, *G. x gaudichaudii* is noted for its hardiness and providing quick groundcover.

to 3–4 m. Left to its own devices, the growth may be somewhat open, but occasional pruning back will thicken growth sufficiently to become impenetrable to most weeds.

The oak-like leaves are attractive, especially at the young growth stage, when they are strongly coloured bronze-red. Though they are slightly prickly, this should not prove a deterrent to gardeners keen to grow this versatile groundcover.

The flowers are a deep wine-red colour and are of the typical toothbrush type. Produced for several months from winter through spring and into early summer, they are carried terminally on vigorous, long branches, so are well displayed.

This is a very versatile plant for groundcover and for spilling over rockeries and walls. It has also been used as a weeping standard grafted onto *G. robusta* rootstock but is not as attractive as the more frequently used 'Royal Mantle' for this purpose. It may be grown in most well-drained soils, in sun or partial shade. Resistant to salt spray and frost-hardy to at least –6°C.

H: 15 cm	Frost-hardy
F: Winter–spring	

Grevillea glabrata

This often-overlooked species from southern Western Australia has a number of landscape applications and other uses that should earn it consideration for a place in many gardens. Reaching a height of 2–3 m, it has an attractive semi-weeping habit that can be encouraged and enhanced with judicious pruning. It may be used as a specimen, as a screening plant, or even kept clipped to form a very graceful hedge.

The distinctive deep green foliage is smooth and wedge-shaped, and provides an appealing foil for the massed displays of lacy white flowers produced for much of the year but especially over winter and spring.

G. glabrata is easily grown in most well-drained soils, being frost-hardy and adaptable to both sun and semi-shade.

H: 2–3 m	Attracts birds
F: Winter–spring	Cut foliage
Frost-hardy	

Grevillea glabrata, a graceful species with a semi-weeping habit, is frost-hardy and versatile.

Grevillea 'Honey Gem'

This outstanding cultivar is yet another example of *Grevillea banksii* passing on its valuable characteristics to its progeny. A natural hybrid of this species with *G. pteridifolia*, this vigorous shrub may reach a height of 5 m but should be pruned regularly to maintain a compact, manageable habit.

The fine, fishbone-like foliage, to 30 cm long, is a deep green with silvery undersides and is similar to the *G. pteridifolia* parent.

The spectacular flower racemes are a vivid golden-orange shade, up to 17 cm long and are borne prolifically for much of the year in warm climates. As with so many grevilleas, these flowers are relished by nectar-seeking birds.

'Honey Gem' has become a widely used feature in both public and private gardens in tropical Australia, especially its native Queensland, and is rapidly gaining popularity in other warm climates around the world. The requirements for successful cultivation are full sun, reasonably well-drained soil and the absence of frost.

H: 5 m	Frost-tender
F: Year-round	Attracts birds

ABOVE: 'Honey Gem' has become a popular landscaping subject in many tropical parts of the world.

BELOW: By either name, *G. hookeriana* 'hybrid' or 'Robin Hood', this is a hardy, prolifically flowering cultivar of great versatility.

Grevillea hookeriana 'hybrid'

(syn. *G.* 'Robin Hood')

This interesting cultivar is sold in Australia as *G. hookeriana* hybrid and in New Zealand as 'Robin Hood'. The true species is not widely cultivated, the hybrid form being preferable for its vigorous habit and very colourful flowers.

It is a dense shrub, reaching a height of 3 m with a greater spread. The rich green fern-like foliage sets off the bright red 80 mm long toothbrush flowers, which are displayed from winter to early summer. These are appreciated by nectar-seeking birds, especially over colder months.

A very suitable and rapid-growing screen plant, *G. hookeriana* 'hybrid' is sometimes grown commercially for its attractive cut foliage. It is easily cultivated in most free-draining soils and in a wide range of climates. Frost-resistant to at least –7°C, it also tolerates coastal conditions well.

H: 3 m	Attracts birds
F: Winter–early summer	Cut foliage
Frost-hardy	

G. juniperina is perhaps the hardiest grevillea, withstanding frost to –20°C. It also clips well to form a colourful hedge.

Grevillea juniperina

This is an extremely variable grevillea from which a number of natural and horticultural forms and hybrids have been marketed. It can vary from a prostrate groundcover to more shrubby habit of 2 x 2m.

The foliage is notoriously prickly, the needle-like bright green (sometimes variegated) leaves being 10–30 mm long and sharply pointed. This species has been used as an animal-proof hedge.

The spider flowers of *G. juniperina* are as variable as its growth habit, ranging in colour from yellow to red with many intermediate shades. Carried as dense clusters to 40 mm wide, they can appear at different times, though winter and spring are most common. They are rich in nectar and supply birds with an abundant source of winter food.

The hardiness and adaptability of this species and its many cultivars has resulted in its being used in landscaping situations with demanding conditions such as very poor soils. In fact almost any free-draining soil in a sunny position is suitable for this grevillea, which will also tolerate frosts as low as –20°C.

H: 2 m	Frost-hardy
F: Winter–spring	Attracts birds

Grevillea lanigera 'Mount Tamboritha'

Grevillea lanigera, the woolly grevillea, has given rise to a number of cultivars, some of which are simple variations of the species; others are hybrids, many of which have occurred naturally. 'Mount Tamboritha' is a prostrate form that is a particularly good rockery plant or groundcover. It has a spread of little more than 1 m and has proved very popular in New Zealand.

Grevillea lanigera 'Mount Tamboritha' spreads in colourful fashion in this rock garden.

The characteristic crowded woolly foliage is a feature of this species, and it is notably smaller on the 'Mount Tamboritha' form. The clustered, nectar-rich flowers of this cultivar are especially well displayed on the ends of the short branches, and are the usual pink and cream seen with the species. They are produced for an extended period over winter and spring.

Most well-drained soils and sunny positions suit this grevillea, which is native to New South Wales and Victoria, but heavy frosts may cause damage. Light pruning will help to keep a compact growth habit.

H: 15 cm x 1 m wide	Medium frost-hardy
F: Winter–spring	Attracts birds

Grevillea *lavandulacea*

This well-known and variable species from South Australia and western Victoria has given rise to several hybrids and numerous selected forms by horticulturists, although botanists recognise just two varieties. Typically this is a spreading shrub to 1.5 m wide and 1 m in height. The grey-green leaves are up to 25 mm

Grevillea 'Red Cloud', a *G. lavandulacea* cultivar, thriving in an arid situation under an ancient eucalyptus .

The red flowers of *G. lavandululacea* 'Red Cloud' contrast with the soft grey-green foliage.

long and are slightly hairy and rough on the upper surface. The flowers are usually red and cream, and produced over winter and spring.

The cultivar illustrated here is known as 'Red Cloud' in New Zealand, where it has been widely grown for the last two decades. The foliage is strongly grey-green and provides a striking background to prolific displays of rich red spider flowers.

This grevillea and its variations are usually frost-hardy, easily grown in almost any well-drained soil, tolerant of very dry conditions and useful in a variety of garden situations.

H: 1 m x 1.5 m wide	Frost-hardy
F: Winter–spring	Attracts birds

Grevillea 'McDonald Park'

(syn. *G.* 'Austraflora McDonald Park', 'Highland Laddie')

A useful and colourful cultivar, 'McDonald Park' is believed to be a hybrid between *G. rosmarinifolia* and *G. alpina* and was collected at McDonald Park by the proprietor of Austraflora Nursery. The original names given to some plants tend to become shortened for commercial purposes, and this one is now widely known as simply *G.* 'McDonald Park'. It has also been marketed in New Zealand as 'Highland Laddie'.

Usually a dense, spreading shrub of 20 cm high by some 60 cm in diameter, it may sometimes attain a height of 70 cm. The small, crowded linear leaves are 20 mm long and a dull green colour.

The massed displays of spider flowers are carried in terminal clusters, are a bright red and gold, and are produced over several months from autumn through winter into spring. Nectar-seeking birds are attracted to this food source, especially over winter.

This is a neat shrub suited to rockery uses, but has also been used successfully as a container plant. It should be lightly pruned after flowering, usually in late spring. The main requirements are well-drained soils, sun or partial shade and protection from heavy frost. It is at its best in temperate climates, as warm, humid environments may cause fungal problems.

| H: 20–70 cm | Medium frost-hardy |
| F: Autumn–spring | Attracts birds |

Grevillea 'Misty Pink'

Yet another hybrid of *G. banksii*, in this case with *G. sessilis*, this delightful and significantly different cultivar was raised at a Queensland nursery and has proved very popular with warm-climate gardeners. 'Pink Surprise' is a similar cultivar. Growth habit is dense, reaching to a maximum of 3 x 3 m, and some pruning is desirable to retain a compact habit.

The large grey-green divided foliage is typical of this hybrid's origins and makes a perfect foil for the spectacular flowers. These are cylindrical racemes to 15 cm long and are pale pink with long cream styles. Blooms can be seen on the bushes at any time of year, with flushes occuring in spring and autumn. They are well displayed and attract nectar-seeking birds.

While 'Misty Pink' will tolerate the occasional light frost, it should be grown in well-drained soils in sunny positions.

| H: 3 m | Tolerates light frosts |
| F: Year-round | Attracts birds |

Grevillea robusta

Silky oak, southern silky oak, he-oka, oka-kilika, ha'iki, ke'oke'o

An Australian native ultimately forming a stately tree up to 35 m high, this tallest grevillea (and best known of the Proteaceae) produces massed displays of large, rich golden-orange toothbrush-like flowers, up to 12 cm long, during spring. These are attractive to nectar-seeking birds and are shown to perfection against the large, light green ferny leaves. Although it can take many years to flower in some colder climates, *G. robusta* is a fast-growing tree and surprisingly frost-hardy, to –8°C. It may become semi-deciduous under such conditions and also during droughts.

The common name silky oak refers to the oak-like

'McDonald Park' is a colourful grevillea with a neat habit, making it suitable for smaller gardens

Grevillea 'Misty Pink' is a popular choice in warmer climates.

timber, which has a silky texture when freshly split. It is used as a timber tree in Malaysia and parts of Africa, and has been used for such purposes as casks, kegs and milk buckets as well as in coachbuilding and cabinet work. This grevillea is grown as a house plant while young in colder countries, and even as a shade tree in African coffee plantations. It is a species widely recognised for its suitability as an amenity tree and is used in roadside plantings and in parks. Large numbers have been planted in forest reserves in Hawaii, where this species is known by several common names.

H: To 35 m	Frost-hardy
F: Spring	Attracts birds

LEFT: *Grevillea robusta*, the silky oak, provides a dazzling display during spring.

Grevillea 'Robyn Gordon'

'Robyn Gordon' is one of the most significant and best grevillea hybrids. The first of the many crosses between *G. banksii* and *G. bipinnatifida*, this outstanding cultivar from the late 1960s forms a shrub of 1.5 m high by 3 m across, but thrives on pruning to maintain a more compact habit if this is desired. It will even spring into vigorous new growth when cut back to a stump.

The large, shiny green, irregularly lobed leaves may be as large as 16 x 13 cm and are a characteristic of this lovely grevillea. The handsome cylindrical flower racemes may measure 15 cm or more in length. They are a rich pinkish red, produced year-round and are attractive to a wide range of nectar-seeking birds.

Suitable as a specimen in warmer climates, 'Robyn Gordon' can also be used very effectively in containers.

'Robyn Gordon' flowers year-round in mild climates.

It performs equally well in both sun and and semi-shade, tolerates the occasional light frost and appreciates moisture provided drainage is adequate. Very dry conditions will stunt growth.

H: 1.5 m	Tolerates light frosts
F: Year-round	Attracts birds

Grevillea rosmarinifolia

Rosemary grevillea

A very well-known and variable grevillea, with many natural hybrids and selected forms being widely grown for decades, *G. rosmarinifolia* is typically a dense shrub up to 2 m high with small, narrow leaves. Among the better-known cultivars are 'Desert Flame', 'Jenkinsii', 'Lara Dwarf', 'Lutea', 'Nana' and 'Pink Pixie'.

Flowers are produced in terminal clusters over winter and spring, with some evident during autumn. They are multi-coloured, with red and pink dominant and the perianth having a cream tip. Some cultivars are appealing to birds.

This grevillea, originating in the south-east of Australia, and its many cultivars are usually hardy to –10°C and easily grown in most well-drained soils and in full sun or semi-shade. Apart from 'Desert Flame', which is best suited to dry, sunny sites, the rosemary grevillea hybrids and cultivars make few demands on the home gardener.

H: 2 m	Frost-hardy
F: Autumn–spring	Attracts birds

The rosemary grevillea is a very variable, hardy, long-lived and reliable species.

Grevillea 'Superb'

Of similar parentage to *G.* 'Robyn Gordon' (*G. banksii* x *G. bipinnatifida*), except that the white form of *G. banksii* was used in the cross-pollination. 'Superb' has a bushy habit of growth to approximately 1.5 m high and is less spreading than 'Robyn Gordon'. Foliage is similarly large and irregularly lobed, but the large flowers differ in being a soft orange shade. 'Mason's Hybrid' (syn. 'Ned Kelly') is a similar cross but with paler flowers.

'Superb' is notably more frost-hardy than 'Robyn Gordon' and is a very reliable cultivar, being long-lived and resistant to pests and diseases. It is a beautiful shrub, well suited to a variety of situations, from shrub borders to specimen uses, and withstands quite hard pruning to maintain a compact habit.

Most well-drained soils suit this grevillea, which is tolerant of frost to –3°C. Even when damaged by colder temperatures it will often spring back into new growth with warmer weather. It performs well in dappled shade as well as full sun. 'Superb' is very popular with nectar-seeking birds.

H: 1.5 m	Tolerates light frosts
F: Year-round	Attracts birds

'Superb' is one of a range of spectacular cultivars but is hardier than most of its relatives.

G. thelemanniana is spectacular when used to fall over a steep bank or wall.

Grevillea thelemanniana

Spider net grevillea, lace net grevillea

There are several recorded forms and subspecies of the spider net grevillea, which is native to the south of Western Australia. Most popular are the groundcover forms cultivated in Australia and also New Zealand, England and the United States.

This grevillea is especially notable for its soft grey-green, net-like foliage – bright green in some cases – and vividly contrasting 70 mm long, rich red toothbrush flowers, which are produced throughout autumn, winter and spring. Although not seen as often under cultivation, there are also orange and pink forms. The commonly grown prostrate form is an excellent hanging subject or 'spiller' for walls, banks and rockeries. It reaches little more than a few centimetres in height, but it can spread up to 2 m or more, and examples may be seen cascading down a wall to as much as 3 m. Light pruning will encourage a more branched habit.

G. thelemanniana is easily grown in well-drained, sunny positions. The common prostrate grey-leaved form is not particularly frost-hardy, being damaged at temperatures much below –2°C. However, it is resistant to salt spray.

H: 10 cm x 2.5 m wide	Tolerates light frosts
F: Autumn–spring	Attracts birds

77

Grevillea venusta

Rusty grevillea

Grevillea venusta has only been introduced to the home gardener in the last few years but has already proved very successful because of its unusual flowers and adaptability to varying conditions.

This is a fast-growing, rounded bush of up to 4 m high with an equal spread with maturity. The large leaves are dark green with prominent paler veins. The flowers are well displayed in terminal racemes throughout the year and are a striking colour combination of long blue-black styles tipped with maroon, while the perianth shades from bright green to yellow at the tip. They are attractive to nectar-seeking birds.

As a native of Queensland, it appreciates full sun, but it is adaptable to a wide range of soils.

H: 4 m	Frost-tender
F: Year-round	Attracts birds

An old favourite, *G. victoriae* is attractive to nectar-seeking birds and is a hardy shrub for a range of situations.

No other grevillea has such unusual flower colouring as *G. venusta*.

Grevillea victoriae

Royal grevillea, mountain grevillea

This well-known grevillea has been cultivated by gardeners for many years and, although not one of the showiest species, it is valued because of its attractive foliage and form, as well as its hardiness and reliability.

It occurs naturally in southern New South Wales and northern Victoria.

The royal grevillea usually forms a neat, dense shrub of up to 2.5 m high with a spread of 1.5–2m. Smooth grey-green leaves provide an attractive background for the 70 mm long, brick-red hanging flowers. Varieties with pink or yellow flowers can also be found. All of the colour forms have similarly shaped flowers that are well displayed and are usually produced during winter and spring and into early summer, providing welcome food for nectar-seeking birds. One form, 'Genoa River', produces blooms all year round.

There are several forms of this grevillea, all of which are frost-hardy. It is well suited for background or screening purposes, but may be lightly pruned to shape to form a neat specimen. This species needs well-drained soils in either full or filtered sun.

H: 2.5 m	Frost-hardy
F: Winter–spring	Attracts birds

HAKEA

There are more than 130 species of this genus, and they may be found in almost all parts of the Australian continent except the rainforests. Foliage is extremely variable, ranging from soft and willow-like, to needle-like to broad and smooth, while others are large and prickly. The seed-bearing woody fruits are also very variable in appearance, some being beak-shaped, others have crests or may look like clubs.

A few hakeas have adapted so well to foreign environments that they have become 'escapees' and been classified as noxious weeds. South Africa in particular has a problem with *Hakea suaveolens, H. sericea* and *H. gibbosa*, which have become invasive and pose a threat to native flora in many areas. An indigenous fungus is making some inroads against these pests, and some weevil species that attack hakea seed have been introduced to assist control.

Hakeas have not been accorded the recognition they deserve, though many are excellent garden plants and will often thrive in difficult positions where little else may survive. Only a few can become problem plants, and a large number are attractive shrubs whose spectacular flowers (mainly the red ones) attract birds.

Hakea bucculenta

Red pokers

This is one of the more spectacular hakea species. It ultimately forms a bushy shrub 4 m high by 3 m across and has both neat foliage and striking flower spikes. Although *Hakea buccxulenta* naturally grows in thickets in very free-draining sandy soils in coastal Western Australia, it can be cultivated in more humid environments provided the all-important perfect drainage is provided.

The rich green, narrowly linear leaves can be up to 17 cm long and show off the handsome red flowers to perfection. The racemes may be 15 cm long and are produced in crowded groups over late winter and spring. Although carried on old wood, they are easily

Hakea bucculenta is a spectacular sight during spring.

The pincushion hakea is a very ornamental species that can be used successfully in a variety of situations.

Hakea multilineata is appealing for its unusual foliage and striking flowers, which are also attractive to birds.

visible through the open foliage, thus attracting nectar-seeking birds.

H. bucculenta is frost-tolerant to about –5°C, and it has been grafted onto *H. salicifolia* rootstock, which has radically improved its adaptability to heavier soils. It may be lightly pruned to keep it more compact.

H: 4 m	Medium frost-hardy
F: Late winter–spring	Attracts birds

Hakea laurina

Pincushion hakea

This species, with its appropriate common name, is probably the best-known ornamental hakea. It bears attractive, unusual flowers, the foliage is sometimes preserved for floral art uses, and it has been used as an ornamental hedge and even as a street tree. Pruned to shape, it can be an attractive specimen in the garden.

The elliptical deep green leaves have prominent veins and are up to 150 mm in length. Young growth is a soft golden-bronze shade, while old foliage can become a rich orange or red before falling. Flowers are a feature of *H. laurina*, forming multi-coloured pincushions of golfball size. They open from pale-cream buds to become red with protruding pin-like styles of a cream shade. At maturity the overall appearance is of a mass of red pincushions during autumn and winter.

This species is widely cultivated outside its native Western Australia. It will tolerate a range of well-drained soils, withstand frost to –5°C and adapt to both humid and dry climates. It is not deep-rooted so may need a reasonably sheltered position.

H: 3 m	Medium frost-hardy
F: Late winter–spring	Attracts birds

Hakea multilineata

Grass-leaf hakea

This attractive species from the south of Western Australia is often confused with several other hakeas, notably *H. francisiana*. This large shrub grows to 5 m high in nature, but is usually smaller under cultivation.

Its narrow, dark green, grass-like leaves can be up to 20 cm long. The erectly held flowers, up to 7 cm long, are a rich pink shade and attract birds. They are produced during spring and are followed by unusual grey fruit with a distinctive upturned 'beak'. These are sometimes used to good effect in dried-flower arrangements.

The grass-leaf hakea is an attractive shrub that is worthy of consideration by gardeners. Good drainage and air circulation in sunny positions sheltered from heavy wind are the main requirements for its successful cultivation. It is tolerant of occasional frosts to about –5°C.

H: 5 m	Medium frost-hardy
F: Spring	Attracts birds

Hakea saligna 'Gold Medal'

This seedling variant displays prominent leaf variegation. Young growth is a deep pink, gradually becoming light pink and cream before maturing to cream and green. The overall effect, especially during spring, is of a bush with a pink halo. Leaves are soft and willow-like.

'Gold Medal' has a dense growth habit to 3 m or more in height with a 2 m spread. It stands up to pruning well and makes an attractive hedge. The creamy-white flowers are small and insignificant, the plant being primarily grown for the foliage. It is also a very suitable subject for screening purposes.

A handsome variegated shrub, 'Gold Medal' is a particularly hardy hakea with many uses.

For a variegated plant, this hakea is surprisingly frost-tolerant, withstanding temperatures as low as –7°C without significant damage. Native to coastal New South Wales, it is easily grown in most soils, whether moist or dry, adapts to both shade and sun and is usually wind-tolerant.

H: 3+ m	Medium frost-hardy
F: Spring	

Hakea victoria

Royal hakea

Named in honour of Queen Victoria, this very distinctive hakea has been described as the most beautiful foliage plant of the protea family. This extraordinary species has large and leathery, brightly coloured leaves, which are prominently veined and have prickly, wavy margins. They are initially green, lower ones becoming bright yellow in the first year, orange the next, until, in the third year when the leaves are lower on the branches, they become a vivid red. As a result, all three colours

The royal hakea is regarded as one of the most beautiful foliage plants.

are seen at once, giving a delightful graduated effect. Cream flowers are borne on pink stems in the leaf axils in spring.

This species in nature forms an erect shrub of 2.5 m but is usually bushier under cultivation. Leaf colouring is often much less prominent in good garden soils.

Usually frost hardy to –3°C, the royal hakea requires perfect drainage and full sun.

H: 2.5 m	Tolerates light frosts
F: Spring	

ISOPOGON

This intriguing genera comprises 34 species and three varieties. The species found naturally in Western Australia are referred to as cone flowers, while those in the eastern states are known as drumsticks. The more spectacular western species are inclined to be more difficult to cultivate than the hardy easterners.

Most isopogons are erect-growing shrubs to 2 m or less, though there are several prostrate species. Some have lignotubers, which enable the plants to regenerate from the rootstock if burnt by bush fires or damaged in some other way. The distinctive flowers are

'Woorikee 2000', the recently introduced dwarf cultivar of *Isopogon anemonifolius* has proved popular as a tub plant.

borne as dense cones, with the blooms radiating from and surrounding the central cone. Some of the western species are prized as cut flowers and are grown commercially. It is probably the rather specific nature of their cultivation requirements that has prevented their being exploited to a greater extent.

Isopogon anemonifolius

Broad-leaf drumstick

This is usually a bushy shrub ranging in height from 50 cm to 2 m, depending on the degree of exposure to wind. There is a low, almost prostrate selection that has achieved popularity as both a rockery subject and a container plant.

The fine, much-divided, bright green leaves are very characteristic of this species and provide a dense background to the vivid yellow cone flowers, which are produced in profusion over spring and early summer in most cases, although in some instances they may commence in late winter.

The dwarf, semi-prostrate cultivar 'Woorikee 2000' will possibly become the most widely grown form of this species. Its compact, mounding habit to less than 30 cm high and with a greater spread has already endeared it to gardeners, especially those with limited space. Spectacular as a patio plant in tubs, especially the popular terracotta types, this cultivar is very free-flowering and easily grown.

Most average, well-drained soils suit this isopogon, which will flower more profusely in full sun. It is tolerant of frosts to –5°C and resistant to salt spray.

H: 0.5–2 m	Frost-hardy
F: Spring	

Isopogon dawsonii

Nepean conebush

In nature *I. dawsonii* forms a tall, open shrub of up to 6 m high, but under cultivation is more usually a bushy shrub of 2 m. A little judicious pruning will ensure a neat, compact habit.

The handsome deeply divided dark green leaves often have a bronze cast and are a feature of the shrub. They provide a contrasting foil for the well-displayed cream-coloured flowers, which appear from late winter through the spring months. These may be up to 40 mm in overall width and are carried terminally.

This isopogon displays more subtle colourings and

is perhaps more of a collector's or connoisseur's plant, but it can look especially handsome when used as an accent plant for foliage variation in a shrub border.

It is usually frost-hardy to –5°C, adaptable to both humid and dry climates, can be grown in sun or semi-shade and tolerates most well-drained soils.

H: 2 m	Frost-hardy
F: Late winter–spring	

Isopogon latifolius

This is the most spectacular *Isopogon* species. It is unfortunately inclined to be temperamental under cultivation, requiring perfect drainage and resenting humid conditions. Its natural habitat – it grows in the Stirling Ranges of Western Australia in sandy soils, often among rocky outcrops – should be considered when attempting to cultivate this species. It is grown successfully as a commercial crop in parts of South Australia in acid, sandy soils and can also be seen in gardens in parts of coastal southern Victoria.

Forming a bushy shrub of up to 2 m, *I. latifolius* has large, bright green leaves to 10 cm or more in length. The flower heads are the largest of the isopogons, measuring an impressive 80 mm or more in overall width, and are a spectacular mauve-pink colour. They are borne in profusion from late winter into spring, and are superb as cut flowers.

Full sun and an acid, very free-draining soil are essential to successful cultivation. Light frosts only are tolerated and humid conditions can cause fungal problems and collapse of the plant.

H: 2 m	Tolerates light frosts
F: Late winter–spring	Cut flowers

KNIGHTIA

Knightia excelsa

Rewarewa, New Zealand honeysuckle tree

New Zealand has two living Proteaceae genera, *Knightia* (rewarewa) and *Toronia* (which is closely related to *Persoonia*). However, these represent only a fraction of the rich and diverse Proteacean flora that inhabited the New Zealand region when it was a low-lying landmass with a subtropical climate similar to that of present-day New Caledonia. From the evidence of fossil leaves

Handsome foliage and creamy-white flowers combine to make *Isopogon dawsonii* a desirable garden plant.

Isopogon latifolius is a stunning species for gardens with light, free-draining soil.

83

and pollen, *Knightia* has been in New Zealand since the Eocene, around 40 million years ago. Between the Eocene and Miocene periods, New Zealand was also home to at least a dozen different Proteacean genera. These included *Adenanthos*, *Banksia*, *Beauprea*, *Carnarvonia*, *Embothrium*, *Isopogon*, *Orites*, *Petrophile*, *Symphonema*, *Telopea* and *Xylomelum*. There are also many other Proteacean pollen types that are not closely related to living plants.

Knightia is a genus of just two species, one of which is found in New Caledonia and the other, better known one in the North Island and upper South Island of New Zealand. While the foliage is superficially similar to *Macadamia*, the flowers and growth habit differ markedly. It is more closely related to the Australian *Darlingia* and *Cardwellia* and New Caledonian *Eucarpha*.

K. excelsa is an erect-growing tree of 30 m when mature. The deep green, coarsely toothed leaves are up to 15 cm long on mature trees and to 25 cm on juvenile plants. They have a distinctive reddish-brown tomentum (matted woolly down) on the undersides. The reddish-brown flowers are particularly distinctive, having a spidery, soft velvet appearance and, as the buds split open to reveal the stamens, they curl back in striking fashion. They are arranged along a central stem and the total flower mass may be 10 cm long and 5 cm in diameter. During summer in their natural habitat these nectar-rich blooms attract tui (parson bird) and korimako (bellbird). Rewarewa timber is attractively grained and has been used in a variety of applications, especially inlay work, parquet floors and picture frames.

Most average, well-drained soils suit this distinctive member of the *Proteaceae*. Some protection during establishment is desirable, but mature trees will withstand frost and even light snowfalls.

H: To 30 m	Frost-hardy
F: Summer	Attracts birds

LEUCADENDRON

This widely cultivated genus of South African shrubs consists of some 80 species and numerous subspecies and cultivars. Found exclusively in the flora-rich Cape region, they have the sexes on separate plants (dioecious) and have distinctive, usually colourful, terminal leaves (bracts) that surround the true flowers.

A large number of species and cultivars have been grown for the commercial cut-flower trade in several countries, the best known being the New Zealand-raised cultivar 'Safari Sunset'. In the past, large volumes of leucadendron material were shipped from South Africa to Europe in particular, where it was sold on flower markets as 'Cape Greens' and treated as long-lasting backing material in floral arrangements. This approach has changed with the realisation that many leucadendron blooms are spectacular flowers in their own right and, as a result, their value and the demand for them have increased dramatically.

All leucadendrons require well-drained, acidic soils and sunny positions in the garden if they are to thrive and produce the colourful bracts for which they are famed. The majority provide excellent winter colour in gardens, *L. laureolum* and *L. salignum* cultivars and 'Safari Sunset' being some of the best for this purpose.

Knightia excelsa, rewarewa, is one of only two New Zealand members of the Proteaceae.

RIGHT: The female form of *Leucadendron argentum*, the Cape silver tree, produces extraordinary seed cones.

Leucadendron album

Linear-leaf conebush

This species is one of the silver conebushes of this sub-section of the leucadendrons. A compact shrub up to 2 m high, it is not often seen in cultivation but is very worthy of a place in the garden.

The foliage is exceptionally beautiful, being fine-textured, soft and a bright silver colour. This provides a stunning foil for the large silvery-pink seed cones. These may be 30 mm or more in diameter and are carried on sturdy stems. They form after the early-summer flowering, and by winter are fully developed. They can persist on the bush for a year or two before the seeds are eventually released, usually in nature by fire. Male flowers are less spectacular, being a pale yellow colour, but they do have a faint pleasant scent.

This leucadendron should have excellent potential for floristry purposes as well as being a delightful smaller shrub for the garden. In the past it has proved difficult to propagate, but modern nursery methods should ensure its availability. It is not difficult to grow, most well-drained, sunny sites proving suitable, and it is frost-hardy to at least –5°C once established.

H: 1–2 m	Frost-hardy
F: Summer	Cut flowers

Leucadendron album has attractive silver foliage and ornamental seed cones.

'Amy' is a neat and colourful leucadendron suited to smaller gardens.

Leucadendron 'Amy'

This charming and popular New Zealand cultivar was developed by television gardening personality, plant breeder and curator of the Auckland Botanic Gardens, Jack Hobbs. He named it for his daughter Amy, now a landscape architecture student.

A manipulated hybrid of *L. 'Julie'* x *L. laureolum* (selected male form) carried out in 1989, this extremely free-flowering leucadendron creates an arresting sight when it is smothered in colourful bracts. These commence as a deep red in autumn, gradually developing cream inner bracts in early spring as the central cone develops. These eye-catching bicolour flowers are a medium size, to about 60 mm wide, and are suitable for picking for smaller arrangements, posies or infill material. Mature bushes will reach to 1.5 x 1m and are excellent garden plants.

This hardy cultivar withstands midwinter frosts to –5°C once established. Most well-drained soils in sunny positions should suit, and it is generally wind-tolerant.

H: 1.5 m	Frost-hardy
F: Winter–spring	Cut flowers

The male flower buds nestle in attractive fashion in *Leucadendron argenteum* foliage.

Leucadendron argenteum

Cape silver tree, silver tree

Famed for its spectacular foliage, *Leucadendron argenteum* has large, broadly pointed green leaves covered in silver silken hairs. These leaves create a vivid display as they shimmer in the wind. A fast-growing small tree to some 10 m and densely foliaged when growing under ideal conditions, it has long branches that are prized in the cut-foliage market. When grown specifically for this purpose and picked heavily, *L. argenteum* becomes a squat, dense shrub and produces more pickable material at an accessible level. In its native habitat, on the slopes of Table Mountain in South Africa's Cape Province, silver trees are usually quite sparsely foliaged and straggly. Cultivated specimens are usually much more lush in appearance.

As with all *Leucadendron* (and *Aulax*) this species has unisexual flowers borne on separate male and female plants (dioecious). The female flowers are ultimately displayed as large, silver, egg-like cones, which carry black seeds on hairy 'parachutes' for wind dispersal. Male flowers are yellow and orange, and are vividly reflected in the surrounding silver bracts.

More than most *Leucadendron* species *L. argenteum* requires very well-drained, lighter soils. It is also quite

Specialist nurseries occasionally offer large specimen examples of *L. argenteum*.

frost-tender while young, but established trees can withstand temperature drops to –4°C. This is an ideal subject for coastal gardens.

| H: 10 m | Tolerates light frosts |
| F: Spring–early summer | Cut foliage |

Leucadendron 'Bell's Sunrise'

(syn. 'Wilson's Wonder')

Originating from the same New Zealand stable during the 1960s as the famed 'Safari Sunset', 'Red Gem' and other leucadendron cultivars, this male selection from the *L. salignum* x *L. laureolum* series of crosses was carried out during this period.

'Bell's Sunrise' is a dense, bushy, sometimes spreading shrub to 1.5 m high with an equal or greater width. The distinctive medium-sized creamy-yellow bracts are flushed with red and surround the central rich yellow flower mass. Stems are frequently multi-headed, adding further to the massed appearance of this floriferous cultivar. Flowering occurs from late winter into spring and while its cut-flower potential is limited because of the habit of male leucadendron flowers blackening quickly, 'Bell's Surprise' is grown for local markets.

This is a lovely cultivar for larger rockeries and shrub borders, its bushy yet compact habit and colourful bracts ensuring it of a place in many gardens. It is usually trouble-free and easy to cultivate in most well-

'Cloudbank Ginny' provides striking colour contrasts.

drained, sunny positions. Frosts to as low as –6°C appear to cause no problems.

| H: 1.5 m | Frost-hardy |
| F: Late winter–spring | Cut flowers |

Leucadendron 'Cloudbank Ginny'

This male cultivar was raised by an Hawaiian nurseryman, the name coming from his nursery, Cloudbank, and his wife, Ginny. The cross is *L. gandogeri* x *L. discolor*, and it has the appearance of a giant colourful *L. discolor*. It has been incorrectly published and sold in New Zealand as 'Cloudbank Jenny'.

A sprawling bush of up to 2 m with an equal spread, it has the unfortunate habit of a percentage of flowering stems having distinct twists and bends, thus making them unsuitable for commercial picking. Floral artists and ikebana exponents do not find this a disadvantage. Spectacular cream bracts surround the bright orange male flowers, which are produced during spring.

Similar improved hybrid cultivars have recently been selected in South Africa and are being marketed there and in Australia and New Zealand under the names 'Red Robin' and 'Spring Red'. They have a more compact, 'squat' habits and are reputed to have the desired straight stems.

Apart from an attraction to caterpillars, this is a trouble-free cultivar, happily adapting to most well-drained, sunny positions and tolerating frosts to –3°C.

'Bell's Sunrise' is a colourful, bushy leucadendron that is noted for hardiness and reliability.

| H: 2 m | Medium frost-hardy |
| F: Spring | |

Leucadendron conicum

Garden Route conebush

In nature this species may reach to 6 m at maturity, but under cultivation it is more usual to see it as a dense, bushy shrub of 2.5 x 2.5m. Although it is not widely cultivated, *L. conicum* has some useful attributes that make it well worth considering.

It is a fast-growing, dense subject, making it very suitable as a screening plant, and its fine, silvery-green foliage can provide an attractive contrast to other shrubs. Autumn growth is often flushed an attractive bronze-pink colour, adding further to the appeal of the foliage. Long stems carry a large number of small flower bracts and can be useful picking, providing nice background or infill material. In the case of the male form, picking at the tight cone stage will enable them to be dried successfully, and the cones often become a charming violet blue.

Easily grown in most free-draining soils, in sun or partial shade, this hardy species will survive frosts to about −7°C when established. It has the additional advantage of being able to be trimmed to create a neat, pyramidal form.

| H: 2.5 m | Frost-hardy |
| F: Spring | Cut flowers |

Leucadendron 'Corringle Gold'

This Australian-raised male cultivar is a *L. gandogeri* x *L. spissifolium* hybrid and has unusual variegated foliage with a predominance of yellow tones surrounding a green central stripe. This is particularly obvious during autumn and winter, and the bright yellow male flower produced in the centre of the creamy-yellow bracts during late winter and spring adds further to the colourful display. As the foliage is so colourful over autumn and early winter when very few other yellow leucadendrons are showing colour, it fills a valuable slot. In addition, the good stem length makes for cut-flower potential.

The appealing long-stemmed flowers of the male form of *Leucadondron conicum*.

The unusual variegated 'Corringle Gold' is particularly colourful in late winter and spring.

'Corringle Gold' forms a rounded shrub of 1.5 x 1.5m, is tolerant of most free-draining soils, colours best in sunny positions, and is normally frost-hardy to about –4°C. It is a registered cultivar.

| H: 1.5 m | Medium frost-hardy |
| F: Autumn–spring | Cut flowers and foliage |

Leucadendron 'Cream Delight'

(syn. 'Bell's Cream')

'Cream Delight' is yet another New Zealand-raised hybrid cultivar from the same plant breeder responsible for 'Safari Sunset' and 'Bell's Supreme'. It is of basically similar parentage, being *L. laureolum* x *L. salignum* (cream form). Other cultivars of similar breeding are 'Highlights' from Australia and 'Maui Sunset' and 'Cloudbank's Sunrise' from Hawaii.

A distinctive cultivar, 'Cream Delight' produces large numbers of cream bracts tinged with red.

This leucadendron grows into a densely erect shrub of 2 m, although heavy picking or pruning will see it become bushier. The neat, medium-sized bracts are an ivory-white colour and develop a pink blush with maturity. Stems are medium length, so this plant has cut-flower potential both commercially and for floral art. It is an attractive garden plant but must be well pruned in late spring, when the bracts have lost colour if a compact habit is to be retained.

This is a frost-hardy, reliable cultivar that is easily grown in most well-drained soils and sunny positions. Unfortunately, it is not readily obtainable outside New Zealand at the time of writing.

| H: 2 m | Frost-hardy |
| F: Autumn–spring | Cut flowers and foliage |

Leucadendron discolor

Piketberg conebush

Boasting one of the more striking colour combinations among the species leucadendrons, *L. discolor* has medium-sized cream bracts that, in male plants, surround bright orange-red strawberry-like flower cones. These appear during spring on stems of medium length that have a limited vase life because the flower blackens with a few days. Picking at the early stages of flower development can delay this. An excellent selected form that originated on a cut-flower farm in Bredasdorp, South Africa, is being marketed as 'Red Robin'. There are also female forms with greenish-white bracts surrounding a green cone on longer stems, which have more potential for picking having a good vase life.

This shrub to 1.5–2 m high, with a usually neat, bushy-to-erect habit, is easily grown in most well-drained soils and is frost-tolerant to –4°C. In Australia the male form is often sold as simply 'Red Centre'. From both the home garden and commercial angles, *L. discolor* has tended to be replaced by the cultivar 'Cloudbank Ginny' and now the newer 'Spring Red'. However, both the species and its cultivars are somewhat subject to caterpillar attack, which gardeners need to be aware of and take action against when spotted.

| H: 1.5–2 m | Medium frost-hardy |
| F: Spring | Cut flowers |

Leucadendron galpinii

Hairless conebush, silver balls

Although not often seen in cultivation, this species has been offered by nurseries in several countries over the years. It has a staunch following among floral artists and is used by florists in posies.

L. galpinii forms a neat, densely erect bush to 2 m high and is easily recognised by its small, slightly twisted grey-green foliage. The silver cones of the female plant are popular for floral work, and the sheer number available for picking, or displayed in the garden for months on end from late spring, makes this a desirable species. The male bush carries nondescript pale yellow flowers in spring.

This hardy, easily grown leucadendron is adaptable to most well-drained soils, performs best in sunny positions, withstands frost to at least −5°C and is quite wind-tolerant.

Photograph on page 92

| H: 2 m | Frost-hardy |
| F: Spring–early summer | Cut flowers |

Leucadendron discolor has particularly distinctive colourings that make it instantly recognisable in both the wild and in the home garden.

Leucadendron galpinii is popular with floral artists.

Leucadendron gandogeri

Broad-leaf conebush

A colourful species that is often used for hybridising purposes, *L. gandogeri* has other attributes, not the least of which is its brilliant garden display over late winter. It also has potential for cut-flower purposes, the female forms often having spectacularly large bracts carried on long, sturdy stems.

In this species male forms are generally compact shrubs, little more than 1 m high, while the females tend to be more upright and reach 1.5–2 m.

ABOVE: A large, female form of *Leucadendron gandogeri*.
BELOW: A very free-flowering, bushy, male form.

Both sexes produce bright yellow bracts, with the male displaying its typical fluffy, pollen-bearing flower in the centre of the bracts. An Australian nursery markets a selection of these male plants under the name 'Spring Gold'.

Generally frost-hardy to around –4°C, *L. gandogeri* seems adaptable to most well-drained, sunny positions and is a reliable, easily grown species.

H: 1–2 m	Medium frost-hardy
F: Winter–spring	Cut flowers

Leucadendron glaberrimum subsp. *erubescens*

Red oily conebush

This startlingly coloured subspecies has larger and much brighter coloured foliage than the species. The leaves are a deep reddish-green colour ,while the flower bracts are a vivid red shade and surround yellow flowers during spring in the case of the more sought-after male.

This has proved a difficult plant to grow under cultivation, having a tendency to be shallow-rooted and subject to root rocking and allied problems. This has been overcome by some nurseries by grafting plants onto the more vigorous *L. eucalyptifolium* rootstock, producing a much more reliable and vigorous plant.

This bushy, spreading shrub, less than 1 m high and with a spread of 1.5 m is not demanding in its requirements when plants have been grafted as mentioned above. It appreciates well-drained, sunny positions and is frost-hardy to about –4°C. The biggest disadvantage this spectacular plant has from a horticultural viewpoint is the mouthful of a name!

H: 1 m	Medium frost-hardy
F: Winter–spring	

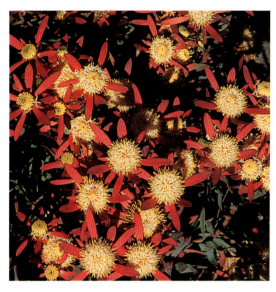

The massed display of late-winter *Leucadendron glaberrimum* subsp. *erubescens*

Leucadendron 'Harvest'

An Australian cultivar, 'Harvest' is a hybrid that originated from a chance seedling of *L. stelligerum*.

Although a male plant with a limited period of flower and bract colour, this cultivar is popular with gardeners for its delightful display over early spring. The bracts are a soft creamy yellow with a strong claret-red flush to the edges, and surround the typical pompom-like male flower of rich yellow. These are produced on short stems, so have only limited picking potential. However, the sheer quantity of flowers makes for a spectacular display, and because blooms virtually smother the compact, rounded bush of only 75 cm high, the overall effect is very pleasing.

'Harvest' is a particularly compact and showy cultivar.

This is a splendid subject for rock gardens, the foreground of shrub borders and in planters. It is usually frost-hardy to about –3°C and is suitable for most well-drained, sunny positions in the garden.

H: 75 cm	Medium frost-hardy
F: Spring	

Leucadendron 'Inca Gold'

One of the most popular bright yellow leucadendron Australian cultivars to be marketed for many years, 'Inca Gold' is presumed to be a cross between *L. laureolum* and *L. salignum* (yellow form). It has a medium-sized bract of a brilliant yellow colour that, combined with a red edge and red stems, provides an exceptionally colourful late-winter to spring display. 'Inca Gold' is a very floriferous cultivar has proven to have good

LEFT: 'Inca Gold' – a free-flowering cultivar that is noted for its frost-tolerance and ease of cultivation.

'Inca Gold' is a popular, hardy leucadendron that gives a colourful display over late winter.

commercial picking potential. Some cut-flower growers experience problems with short stems, but irrigation over summer and early autumn, plus a good pruning programme over mid- to late spring, should overcome this difficulty.

In most garden situations 'Inca Gold' develops a dense, bushy growth habit to 1.5 x 1.5 m, and is usually long-lived and trouble-free. It is hardy to at least –6°C.

H: 1.5 m	Frost-hardy
F: Winter–spring	Cut flowers

Leucadendron 'incisum'

This strangely named cultivar is obviously a selected, prostrate form of *L. salignum*. Originating in New Zealand, where it has been marketed for more than 30 years, *L.* 'incisum' has proved consistently popular with gardeners both for its procumbent habit and distinctively coloured bracts.

The growth habit of this leucadendron is usually no more than 30 cm high, with a slow spread to as much as 2 m. The squat, creamy-white bracts are well displayed over winter, and the colour deepens with age, an orange-bronze flush becoming dominant with the advent of spring. The female flower cone is well displayed.

This is an excellent choice for spilling over banks and walls and can also provide excellent groundcover in shrub borders and similar applications. It is another of the many examples of the extremely variable nature of *Leucadendron salignum*, with *L.* 'incisum' exhibiting the same hardy and reliable characteristics.

H: 30 cm	Frost-hardy
F: Winter–spring	

Leucadendron 'incisum' is an excellent groundcover.

'Julie' is a popular compact cultivar with a profusion of small bracts over winter and spring.

Leucadendron 'Julie'

This New Zealand female cultivar is typical of a particular range of hybrids of *L. salignum* parentage, another very similar example being the Australian-raised 'Baby Bouquet'.

Typically, these cultivars are of tidy, bushy yet erect habit, rarely exceeding 1.5 m in height and producing massed displays in early spring of small cream bracts that are flushed with reddish-bronze tones, especially on the reverse and tips of the bracts. Stem length is not spectacular, usually 30–35 cm, but 'Julie' is very useful for posy work and similar applications.

These cultivars are hardy, withstanding frost and wind, and thriving in a range of soil types. They are usually very reliable and pest- and disease-resistant.

H: 1.5 m	Frost-hardy
F: Late winter–spring	Cut flowers

Leucadendron laureolum

(previously *L. decorum*)

Yellow tulip, golden conebush

L. laureolum has probably been cultivated by gardeners in several countries for longer than any other leucadendron species. In New Zealand, for instance, it has been offered by nurseries for at least 50 years.

This variable species can range in bract colour from pale lemon-yellow to the richest gold shades. Bract size, stem length and growth habit are also very variable. Typically it is a bush of some 2 m with a dense, vigorous habit, and produces large golden bracts on long stems during winter and early spring. Male plants are often less vigorous and have a deeper yellow colour to the smaller bracts.

Two well-known cultivars are the New Zealand selection 'Rewa Gold' and the Hawaiian 'Colin Lennox'. The former has become a significant export crop from New Zealand but is prone to leaf-spotting problems. 'Colin Lennox' is more resistant to pests and diseases, and is a richer golden yellow shade, but probably less productive and throws fewer long stems. It is, however, a more erect shrub.

Frost-hardy to –6°C and generally easy to cultivate, this species must have excellent drainage to thrive and full sun to produce good colour in the bracts.

H: 2 m	Frost-hardy
F: Late winter–spring	Cut flowers

A typical *Leucadendron laureolum* with its massed winter display of brilliant colour.

L. laureolum 'Colin Lennox' is a desirable cultivar with large, deep gold, tulip-shaped bracts.

Leucadendron 'Maui Sunset'

A forerunner to cultivars such as 'Cream Delight' and 'Cloudbank's Sunrise', this hybrid of *L. laureolum* x *L. salignum* origins was raised in Hawaii, as its name suggests, in the early 1980s.

Prone to become a bush of somewhat open and lax habit unless kept well pruned, 'Maui Sunset' usually reaches a height of little more than a metre with a spread of a little less. The medium-sized bracts are a soft greenish white over late winter and early spring, becoming suffused with soft pink shadings as summer approaches. Although this cultivar's short stems, 30–40 cm, limit its commercial picking potential, 'Maui Sunset' has proved popular with home gardeners and floral artists, who appreciate its subtle colouring.

This is a reliable, long-lived leucadendron that is normally frost-hardy to –5°C. Bract colour is more pronounced in full sun, and most free-draining soils seem to suit 'Maui Sunset'.

H: 1 m	Frost-hardy
F: Winter–spring	Cut flowers

RIGHT: 'Maui Sunset' produces handsome white bracts that develop a pink flush as they mature.

Leucadendron orientale

Van Staden's sunbush

L. orientale is an under-rated leucadendron that has excellent potential as a cut flower, using either male or female plants. Both are attractively perfumed, have large bracts and long stems, and flower midwinter to spring.

Closely related to *L. tinctum*, this species forms an erect shrub, 1.5 m high, with bright green foliage, the females having larger leaves. The flower stems may be up to 80 mm or more long and carry the broad, soft yellow bracts that surround either the fluffy male flower or female cone. The latter turns deep red as it matures, and the bracts also assume a red colour. Several selected cultivars are offered by nurseries.

Most well-drained acidic soils are suitable for this appealing leucadendron. A sunny position, sheltered from heavy frost, is desirable, and plants should be pruned or picked to encourage a bushy, compact habit. Tip pruning will encourage a well-branched framework from an early stage.

H: 1.5 m	Tolerates light frosts
F: Winter–spring	Cut flowers

A mature bush of 'Pisa' makes a colourful spring display. Its handsome branches (BELOW) are prized by florists, who also use individual bracts in posies.

Leucadendron 'Pisa'

So named because of its willowy flowering branches that tend to 'lean' in the wind, 'Pisa' is a female hybrid cultivar of *L. floridum* that originated in New Zealand in the late 1970s from seed imported by Geoff Jewell.

This is a vigorous, fast-growing shrub to 2.5 m high with an erect habit. Its slightly twisted silvery-green linear foliage is an identifying character. The well-displayed lime-green bracts surround large silver cones, and several will be found on each of the metre-long flowering branches during late spring to early summer. They pick extremely well over several weeks and last well both in the vase and in transit for exporters.

'Pisa' is frost-hardy and wind-tolerant (including salt-laden winds) but requires a well-drained, sunny positions. It should be well pruned in late spring to encourage new growth and a bushy habit.

H: 2.5 m	Frost-hardy
F: Late spring	Cut flowers

LEFT: *L. orientale* 'Fionaflora' – a spectacular New Zealand-raised female selection.

INSET: 'Scented Petals' – a sweet-scented Australian-raised male selection.

Leucadendron radiatum

Langeberg conebush

Although scarcely seen under cultivation, this charming species should be more widely grown. It has a neat growth habit, to 60 cm, and small, dark green leaves that are thickly twisted and become a purplish tone at the tips, where they become the involucral bracts. These surround purple flower cones in the more attractive female and have potential use for posies.

'Red Gem' as the focal point in a mixed protea garden.

The rarely available *Leucadendron radiatum* is a little delight that is easily grown and very attractive.

L. radiatum is surprisingly frost-hardy and easy to grow in most well-drained sunny sites. Light pruning after flowering will encourage a compact habit.

H: 60 cm	Frost-hardy
F: Early summer	Cut flowers

Leucadendron 'Red Gem'

(known as 'Gem' in Australia)

Another New Zealand-raised hybrid from the same breeder and the same batch of crosses as 'Safari Sunset', this cultivar lacks the visual impact of its close relative but nevertheless has several attributes that make it

worthy of a place in the larger garden. A very similar cultivar is marketed in Australia as simply 'Gem'.

'Red Gem' forms a particularly bushy, dense shrub of 2 m high by 2.5m wide. It often branches to ground level so is an ideal choice for screening purposes or covering a problem bank. The dark green foliage often has a bronze cast, and leaves have a small dark red pointed tip.

The large bracts of this female cultivar form appear in late summer and initially are a deep bronze-red

The bronze-red bracts of 'Red Gem' in early winter.

shade, which lightens as winter progresses until the inner bracts display a cream colour as they flare open from late winter to early spring. Stems are not long, to about 40 cm, which limits cut-flower potential.

An easily grown, frost-hardy and wind-tolerant leucadendron, 'Red Gem' is long-lived and reliable and makes a lovely background subject.

| H: 2 m | Frost-hardy |
| F: Autumn–spring | Cut flowers |

Leucadendron rubrum

(previously *L. plumosum*)

Spinning top

This is another leucadendron species that is not often seen in cultivation, except in connoisseurs' gardens, but deserves to be better known, as it has considerable potential for floral art. The female flower cones can be used at any of the three stages: fresh; the unopened colourful seed cone; or fully opened out at the seed-dispersal stage when the bush dies or the cones are picked and dried. Male flowers are small, soft yellow and fluffy and are borne prolifically on a more densely branched shrub than the female plant.

Forming a neat, erect shrub of 1.5–2 m, this species flowers in early spring and, although not spectacular, could find a place in many gardens. It is generally frost-hardy, drought-resistant and easily grown.

| H: 1.5–2 m | Frost-hardy |
| F: Autumn–spring | Cut flowers |

L. rubrum is an intriguingly different species that has uses in floral art and is a collector's item.

'Safari Goldstrike' ia an interesting long-stemmed cultivar with good cut-flower potential.

Leucadendron 'Safari Goldstrike'

This distinctive female cultivar is reputed to be a hybrid of *L. strobolinum* x *L. laureolum* origins and was developed by a New Zealand nursery in the late 1990s.

A large, dense bush of erect habit, 'Safari Goldstrike' produces metre-long flowering stems, and large, tulip-shaped creamy-white bracts appear during winter to early spring. These gradually flare open to form a cup shape.

This fairly recent introduction is becoming popular with commercial flower growers. While reasonably frost-hardy and wind-tolerant, it must be provided with very free-draining soil and a sunny situation.

| H: 2 m | Frost-hardy |
| F: Winter–spring | Cut flowers |

Leucadendron 'Safari Sunset'

Without doubt, 'Safari Sunset' is the most widely culti-vated leucadendron (species or cultivar) and arguably the most successful proteaceous cut flower to date, with millions of stems being grown in several countries for export. A New Zealand-raised cultivar by Ian Bell, dating to the early 1960s, this cross of *L. laureolum* x *L. salignum* (red form) has proved the significance of hybridising to the protea industry. 'Silvan Red', an Australian-raised cultivar of the same parentage, has a less vigorous growth habit and slimmer stems.

If left unpruned or not picked, 'Safari Sunset' will quickly become a tall (to 3 m), somewhat straggly bush. Heavy picking or a disciplined yearly pruning is essen-tial to maintain a dense, bushy habit. The very rich red bracts form on long stems from late summer, and dur-ing autumn and winter are at their peak for picking purposes. From late winter into spring the bracts spread open to reveal a cream inner, and at this stage are some-times marketed as 'rainbow' or 'tri-colour' leucaden-drons. The combinations of strong colour, extreme stem length (often over 1 m), prolonged vase life and lasting qualities for shipping purposes have provided a cut-flower grower's dream plant.

Most well-drained soils suit 'Safari Sunset', but full sun is essential to achieve maximum bract colour. It is normally frost-hardy to about –6°C.

H: 2–3 m	Medium frost-hardy
F: Autumn–winter	Cut flowers

At the popular late-winter stage of multi-coloured bracts, 'Safari Sunset' is an icon of the protea flower industry.

Leucadendron 'Safari Sunshine'

This intriguing cultivar is a 'sport' from 'Safari Sunset', a branch of that cultivar being observed to have strik-ingly variegated foliage and the resulting propagated material retaining that characteristic. The New Zealand- and Australian-raised cultivars 'Jester', 'Safari Sunshine' and 'Katie's Blush' (the latter a sport of 'Silvan Red') are all fundamentally similar.

Less vigorous than 'Safari Sunset' or 'Silvan Red' these variegated forms rarely exceed 1.5 m in height but tend to be bushier, spreading to a similar width. The foliage and bract colour is the traditional rich red but with a prominent green stripe through the centre. Young growth is predominantly pink.

This very distinctive and hardy cultivar is showy as a garden plant and is being increasingly used as cut-flower and foliage material.

H: 1.5 m	Medium frost-hardy
F: Autumn–winter	Cut flowers and foliage

RIGHT: 'Safari Sunshine' (illustrated here) and the very similar 'Jester' and 'Katie's Blush' are spectacular variegated leucadendron cultivars.

'Safari Sunset' makes a powerful statement over winter.

Leucadendron salignum

Common sunshine conebush

In nature this is the most widespread leucadendron species, being found throughout much of South Africa's Cape. It is also the most variable, with colours ranging from pale creams through rich yellows to brilliant reds. Bract size and shape can range from small and slim to broad and squat, while growth may be almost prostrate, bushy and compact, or tall to 2 m or so. Numerous cultivars are marketed by nurseries, some of which are selections taken from seedlings, while others are manipulated hybrids such as 'Safari Sunset'.

It would require several pages to describe all the cultivars on offer and even then some would be omitted. Some of the better-known and more interesting examples are illustrated here.

A pale cream version of *L. salignum*.

'Red Carpet' is a low-growing red cultivar.

'Winter Red' – an outstanding new Australian cultivar with intensely deep red colouring.

'Mrs Stanley' – a popular *L. salignum* cultivar in its spring colours.

Generally this is a very hardy species, tolerating wind and heavy frost better than most. It is also adaptable to varying soils but has usual cultivation requirements of good drainage and sun.

H: Prostrate– 2 m	Frost-hardy
F: Autumn–spring	Cut flowers

Leucadendron strobolinum

Peninsula conebush

A taller-growing species, to about 2.5 m, *L. strobolinum* forms a sturdy trunk and, because the branches arise from the base, it is usually a shapely shrub.

The broad, dark green foliage is appealing, and the wide bracts vary in colour from ivory to yellow, surround prominent cones or flowers and are produced during early spring. Both male and female plants are attractive, but the female is the more sought after for cut-flower purposes.

A frost-hardy species that is long-lived, trouble-free and adaptable to a range of free-draining soil types.

Photograph on page 106

H: 2.5 m	Frost-hardy
F: Spring	Cut flowers

Leucadendron 'Super Star'

'Super Star' is an interesting male cultivar, a result of natural hybridisation between *L. salignum* and *L. lanigerum*, that has been marketed in New Zealand for at least the past two decades.

This is a particularly broad, dense, bushy shrub, only 1 m high but spreading to 2 m wide. The prolific late winter to spring display comprises starry bracts of red with creamy-yellow inner surfaces, which in turn surround the yellow male flower. These are carried on long fine stems and smother the bush.

While not noted for having great cut-flower potential, this cultivar is occasionally used as filler in floral arrangements and for posies. It is also an ornamental shrub for the foreground of shrub borders and similar applications.

This is a particularly wind- and frost-tolerant shrub that is easily grown in a wide range of well-drained soils and sunny positions. It should be lightly pruned immediately after flowering.

H: 1 m	Frost-hardy
F: Spring	Cut flowers

Prolific flowering is characteristic of 'Super Star'.

Leucadendron tinctum

(Previously *L. grandiflorum*)

Rose cockade

An intriguing species, *L. tinctum* produces large seed cones of deep bronze-red in the case of the female, or yellow flowers in the male. Both are surrounded by broad bracts of golden yellow, which age to ornamental shadings of red. These are produced from midwinter through early spring, creating a continually changing colour pattern as they develop.

A sturdy bush of a little more than a metre in height, this species has been cultivated for many decades by gardeners. While not noted as a cut flower, owing to its

short stem length, its colourful cones and bracts are appreciated by both florists and floral artists.

L. tinctum is regarded as a reasonably frost-hardy and wind-tolerant species that should be easy to cultivate in most free-draining, sunny gardens.

H: 1 m	Medium frost-hardy
F: Winter–spring	Cut flowers

ABOVE: The ornamental male form of *L. tinctum*.

BELOW: The large, rich red female seed cone.

LEFT: The ivory-white bracts of 'Waterlily', a female
L. strobolinum cultivar, typify the appeal of this species.

Leucadendron 'Tokyo Gold'

The number of *Leucadendron* cultivars originating from New Zealand seems to be almost endless. 'Tokyo Gold' is one of the most recent, being released in 2001. It is a seedling plant originally raised by the late Jack Harre and is of *L. strobolinum* parentage.

Initially slow to establish, the bush will ultimately reach 2 m in height with a densely upright growth habit.

The handsome 'Tokyo Gold', a recent New Zealand release,
is of *L. strobolinum* parentage.

The broad, deep green foliage has a dark red margin, and the thick flowering stems are tinged red. The bracts develop over winter and are a pale green colour, changing to pale cream before becoming a bright golden yellow with red edges and tips in late spring. The length of stems is usually in the 50–70 cm range, making it useful for picking purposes.

'Toyo Gold' responds well to pruning in early summer when bract colour has finished, and can be kept to a dense, bushy shape if desired. It makes a handsome garden subject, can be used for picking and is one of the more reliable luecadendron cultivars. It will tolerate winter temperature drops to –6°C and flourishes in most well-drained, sunny positions.

H: 1.5–2 m	Medium frost-hardy
F: Late spring	Cut flowers

Leucadendron xanthoconus

Sickle-leaf conebush

A densely erect shrub, 2.5–3 m high, this leucadendron produces long stems of willowy foliage that terminate

A striking *Leucadendron xanthoconus* cultivar used for commercial picking is 'Patea Gold'. It is used at both the yellow-bract stage in spring (LEFT) and the red-cone summer stage ABOVE).

in colourful yellow bracts over spring. These encase either bright yellow male flowers or the female flower cones, which enlarge and become red-coloured in summer.

This is a lovely picking proposition for both long-stemmed infill material or for stripping off individual sprigs of cone for posy work. As a shrub it also presents possibilities as a fast-growing screening subject or a soft, willowy look in a background plant.

Usually both frost- and wind-tolerant, *L. xanthoconus* is easily grown and reliable in both commercial plantings or the home garden.

H: 2.5–3 m	Medium frost-hardy
F: Spring–early summer	Cut flowers

RIGHT: *Leucadendron* 'Colin Lennox' is a good example of the prolific display of large yellow bracts produced by *L. laureolum* cultivars.

LEUCOSPERMUM

Leucospermum comprises some 48 species, of which all but three are native to South Africa. There are many named cultivars, and intensive breeding programmes in South Africa and Hawaii are producing spectacular hybrids with disease-resistant characteristics. The new cultivars becoming available range from dramatic groundcovers to brilliant long-stemmed flowers produced on large bushes.

Commonly referred to as 'pincushions' or simply 'pins', this genus has become an increasingly significant export cut-flower crop in several countries apart from its native South Africa. As the flowering time is generally from midspring to midsummer in the Southern Hemisphere, export of cut blooms to northern winter and Christmas markets has considerable economic importance. This 'season' is often extended at either end by crops produced in the Northern Hemisphere, such as in Hawaii, which is able to harvest leucospermums several weeks earlier than California, thus giving the island state a distinct export advantage to the mainland United States over its competitor.

LEFT: *Leucospermum* 'Veldfire' is a very free-flowering and reliable *L. glabrum* cultivar.

BELOW: *Leucospermum* 'Caroline' – a popular cultivar.

Leucospermum 'Caroline'

'Caroline' has become a very popular cultivar in several countries, notably New Zealand. It is a hybrid between *L. cordifolium* and *L. tottum* and displays the free-flowering habits of both parents, with a deep orange-red colouring and the smaller foliage of *L. tottum*.

The medium-sized pincushion flower heads occur prolifically from spring to early summer, and the initial colour ages to a deeper carmine-red shade. The bush is of compact habit, usually to 1 x 1 m, occasionally more. Although the flowering stems are not noted for length, this is a popular picking leucospermum with a good vase life.

'Caroline' is an easily grown subject, suiting most sunny, well-drained gardens that are not subject to frosts harsher than –3 or –4°C.

H: 1 m	Attracts birds
F: Spring–early summer	Cut flowers
Medium frost-hardy	

Leucospermum catherinae

Catherine wheel pincushion

This pincushion is a very distinctive species that could not be confused with any other. The extraordinary 150 mm wide flower heads of soft orange with their bent

The very distinctive Catherine wheel pincushion.

styles of mauve-pink resemble a spinning Catherine wheel firework. These are produced in large numbers over early summer and deepen in colour intensity with age.

A bushy shrub to 2.5 x 2.5 m, this species has grey-green foliage with red-tipped teeth to the leaf tips. It is a wind-resistant plant that is well suited to coastal conditions with salt winds and sandy soils, but will perform well in most well-drained sites with ample sun. Frosts to –4°C are tolerated.

H: 2.5 m	Medium frost-hardy
F: Early summer	

Leucospermum cordifolium

(previously *L. nutans*)

The pincushion, 'Sunburst'

This is the best-known leucospermum species under cultivation, with its many cultivars sought after by commercial flower growers and gardeners alike. In nature it is found over a wide area of the south-western Cape in South Africa and is usually a wide-spreading shrub of 2 m x 2 m. Colour of the famed pincushion flower head can vary from pinkish yellow through brilliant oranges to crimson-red.

There are numerous cultivars, some of which are simply named selections of superior forms, while others are manipulated hybrids of great potential with desirable characteristics such as longer, straighter stems, more vivid colours, disease resistance and a range of flowering times. 'Harry Chittick', 'Riverlea', 'Calypso', 'Dawn', 'Copper', 'Sunshine' 'California Sunshine', 'Eldorado', 'Flamespike' and 'Caroline' are just a few of the cultivars that have been marketed over the years.

This leucospermum requires light, well-drained soil and a sunny position if it is to thrive. Open positions with exposure to some wind are not usually a problem and may in fact help keep the bushes healthier than in crowded and sheltered situations. Heavy frost is not tolerated, with about –3°C being the limit before damage occurs.

Photograph right

H: 2 m	Attracts birds
F: Spring–summer	Cut flowers
Medium frost-hardy	

Leucospermum cuneiforme

(previously *L. attenuatum*)

Wart-stemmed pincushion

A widespread species through the southern Cape, *L. cuneiforme* is an attractive and colourful shrub despite its new common name, which refers to the small warty knobs on the base of stems arising from the rootstock.

They do not detract from the plant. In nature this is usually a tall shrub of 2–3 m, but it will often form a more dense, bushy specimen under cultivation. It is a very variable species, and prostrate dwarf forms are also seen in nature. The Hawaiian-raised 'Hawaii Gold' is a cross of *L. cuneiforme* and *L. conocarpodendron*.

The massed displays of large, brilliant golden-yellow pincushion flowers, which age to a soft orange shade, are carried for months from the end of winter through spring to midsummer. They create a spectacular show over this period and, while not as commercial for picking as some leucospermums, are excellent for home arrangements and floral artistry.

This species, like most of the genus, requires light, free-draining soils and open, sunny positions. It is sensitive to hard frost. It will shoot from its rootstock when cut hard back, so can be kept to manageable proportions in smaller gardens. The cultivar 'Goldie', which has more compact, deeper-coloured flowers, is hardier than the usual species.

H: 2–3 m	Attracts birds
F: Spring–summer	Cut flowers
Tolerates light frosts	

RIGHT: *L. cuneiforme* is a brilliantly coloured addition to spring and early-summer gardens.

L. cordifolium 'Riverlea' – a vigorous cultivar suitable for cut-flower and garden purposes.

Leucospermum 'Fantasy'

This distinctive New Zealand-raised cultivar was once erroneously sold as *Leucospermum tottum,* but it is most likely a hybrid between *L. cordifolium* and *L. tottum.* It has been grown by enthusiastic gardeners for more than 20 years.

'Fantasy' is distinguished by long, horizontally arching stems that carry soft salmon-pink heads with a mauve cast. They have the shape of *L. cordifolium* but are nearer to *L. tottum* in colour and can be seen from midspring into summer. Its unusual arching stems have not prevented its use as a cut flower.

The growth of this shrub is usually broadly spreading to 2.5 m or more and up to 2 m in height. It is notably hardy to midwinter temperatures as low as −6°C, requires well-drained soils, will flower nearly as well in filtered shade as full sun, and is normally a long-lived and reliable cultivar.

H: 2 m	Attracts birds
F: Spring–summer	Cut flowers
Frost-hardy	

Leucospermum 'Firefly'

A neat, densely compact growth habit has contributed to the popularity of this very floriferous cultivar. Reputed to be a cross between *L. tottum* and *L. cordifolium,* it has the smaller flower size of the former, with the colouring showing more of the latter's influence. In fact the massed displays of bloom are initially a deep orange-red over spring but darken to a carmine shade as they age on the bush. It is at this stage that the *L. tottum* parentage is apparent. The Australian cultivar 'Firewheel' is similar to 'Firefly'.

Growing to little more than 1 x 1m, this delightful cultivar is sometimes used by florists despite its short stem length. It has great appeal to floral artists and is a very popular garden plant for long-lasting display over spring and summer. Frost-hardy to around −4°C once well established, it withstands wind, benefits from a light pruning after flowering and should be provided with the usual free-draining soil and sunny position.

H: 1 m	Attracts birds
F: Spring–summer	Cut flowers
Medium frost-hardy	

LEFT TOP: 'Fantasy' is an interesting hybrid that has proven to be one of the more frost-hardy leucospermums.

LEFT: The compact, free-flowering and colourful *Leucospermum* 'Firefly'.

Leucospermum 'Flame'

A very appealing cultivar originating in New Zealand in 1980 from *L. lineare* seed imported from South Africa by Geoff Jewell. Because of the differences from the species that it displays, this is more likely a natural hybrid with a species such as *L. cordifolium.*

The long flower stems carry striking clear orange-red flowers, which deepen in colour with maturity. They are produced earlier in the season than many other cultivars, commencing in early spring but carrying on well into summer. With a long vase life, the blooms are highly regarded for commercial picking purposes. Leaves are very narrow, but not as much as the *L. lineare* species. This leucospermum forms a densely erect shrub of 2 m high with a spread of 1.5 m.

'Flame' is a usually trouble-free plant that tolerates frost to –4°C, is vigorous and will grow in most sunny, free-draining parts of the garden.

H: 2 m	Attracts birds
F: Spring–summer	Cut flowers
Medium frost-hardy	

Leucospermum 'Goldie'

'Goldie', reputedly a seedling selection of *L. cuneiforme*, has been available in the nursery trade for at least the past decade but is not often seen, probably because it is more difficult to propagate and slower to grow to a well-branched, saleable plant. In spite of this, it is a very desirable cultivar. It has small domed flower heads of a deep golden yellow that assume rich orange tones with age and are carried on long, slim stems from late spring through midsummer. 'Goldie' is an excellent cut-flower subject and has the benefit of being able to be pruned extremely hard and then shooting away into new growth from the rootstock. It is usually a long-lived and reliable shrub.

This leucospermum will eventually form a much-branched, erect shrub of 2 m but consistent picking will be inclined to keep it more compact, at 1–1.5 m. It is noted for withstanding midwinter temperatures of –5°C once it is well established.

H: 1–2 m	Attracts birds
F: Spring–summer	Cut flowers
Medium frost-hardy	

RIGHT TOP: 'Flame' is an excellent commercial picking cultivar with long stems, bright colour and fine foliage.

RIGHT: 'Goldie' – a desirable, rich golden selection of *L. cuneiforme* that has neat, compact flower heads.

Leucospermum 'High Gold'

At the time of writing, this *L. cordifolium* x *L. patersonii* cultivar bred by the ARC Fybos Unit in South Africa is becoming one of the most popular yellow-flowered leucospermum cultivars on the market. This can be attributed to a number of factors, not the least of which is its particularly robust dark green foliage, which, coupled with a vigorous, erect growth habit, makes for a handsome specimen. It also appears to have good disease resistance.

The foliage provides a striking foil for the clear yellow pincushion flower heads that are borne on long stems from midspring through into summer. As with so many *L. cordifolium* cultivars, 'High Gold' is proving to have excellent picking qualities for commercial flower growers.

Moderately frost-hardy, withstanding the odd mid-winter temperature drop to –5°C, this plant is at its best in well-drained, sunny situations.

H: 1.5 m	Attracts birds
F: Spring-summer	Cut flowers
Medium frost-hardy	

Leucospermum mundii

Langeberg pincushion

This unusual species was until recently not often seen in gardens, but a lower-growing form has become quite popular in Australia, where it is promoted as both a tub plant and a groundcover with a spreading habit and reaching 50 cm in height. In nature it is more normally an erect, branched shrub up to 1 m.

The small flowers are borne in dense terminal clusters over late spring and early summer. They commence as pale yellow and age to deep orange, with all shades present at once, creating a colourful display.

While *L. mundii* is a drought-resistant species, it should be watered well to aid establishment, especially in dry soils. Light frosts and winds are tolerated and sunny positions are preferred.

H: 50 cm – 1 m	Tolerates light frosts
F: Spring–summer	Attracts birds

LEFT TOP: A recent release, 'High Gold' is proving a very popular leucospermum cultivar.

LEFT: The charming *L. mundii* has intrigued many Australian connoisseurs.

Leucospermum oleifolium

Overberg pincushion

Like *L. mundii*, a selected form of this species is promoted in Australia as a groundcover and tub plant growing to 50 cm high, whereas in nature it is usually an erect shrub of 1 m.

The delightful clusters of small flower heads range from pale yellow through orange to deepest crimson, according to age, and all colours may be seen at once on the bush. The extended flowering period occupies at least eight weeks from spring to midsummer.

The Overberg pincushion features a colourful mixture of bloom stages on the plant at the same time.

Hardiness is variable according to the form, but the one marketed in Australia is regarded as withstanding light frosts to about –2 or –3°C. Well-drained soils are essential for successful cultivation, and sun is necessary to ensure prolific and colourful flowering. It is suitable for coastal gardens.

H: 50 cm – 1 m	Tolerates light frosts
F: Spring–summer	Attracts birds

Leucospermum praecox

Small to medium-sized flowers produced much earlier than most other leucospermum species are a characteristic of *L. praecox*. These are clustered, often in groups of four, are up to 60 mm wide and are a bright yellow

L. praecox 'Patricia', a selected form marketed in Australia.

L. prostratum trails over walls effectively and has delightful little scented flowers.

over winter before ageing to dark orange in spring.

A taller shrub, reaching 2 m with maturity, it is very free-flowering and makes a colourful display in the winter and early spring garden. In Australia a selected form marketed as 'Patricia' is popular in coastal gardens. This species is occasionally used for cut-flower purposes but is probably more widely appreciated as an appealing garden subject.

Frost-hardy to at least −5°C, this species is noted for its longevity and ease of cultivation. It is also drought-resistant once established.

H: 2 m	Attracts birds
F: Winter–spring	Cut flowers
Frost-hardy	

Leucospermum prostratum

Yellow trailing pincushion, 'Groundfire'

One of the loveliest of the small-flowered leucospermums, *L. prostratum* is naturally found growing in very acidic, sandy coastal regions, though selected forms under cultivation have proved adaptable to a wide range of well-drained soils.

This prostrate species is ideally suited to spilling over banks and walls, but in some circumstances it will mound to form a dense, cushion-like mass of foliage. More usually it sends out long, trailing stems from its underground rootstock. Regular pruning will encourage a dense growth habit.

The massed displays of little pompom flowers are produced over a long period from late winter to midsummer and are a bright yellow at first, ageing to orange and then red, all colours appearing on the plant together. As an added bonus they have a delightful citrus scent.

Very well-drained soils, sunny positions, protection from all but light frosts and avoidance of fertilisers are prerequisites for success with this little charmer.

H: Prostrate	Tolerates light frosts
F: Winter–summer	

Leucospermum 'Red Sunset'

This *L. lineare* x *L. cordifolium* cultivar shows the equal influence of both parents in foliage and flower, being about halfway between in terms of leaf width and also flower shape and colour.

Yellow-orange flowers are produced on stems of average length, and age subtly to a soft red shade. They have the benefit of flowering earlier than many cultivars, commencing in late winter and carrying on through spring into early summer.

'Red Sunset' is a compact, rounded shrub, to 1.5 x 1.5 m, that requires little or no pruning to maintain a good shape. It is noted for being at home in coastal gardens and will tolerate frost to about −3°C.

H: 1.5 m	Attracts birds
F: Spring–summer	Cut flowers
Medium frost-hardy	

Leucospermum reflexum

Skyrocket pincushion

A particularly dense, bushy shrub that grows up to 4 m, *L. reflexum* is easily recognised by both the small grey-green leaves held closely to the stems, and the spectacular reddish-orange flower heads, which characteristically reflex the styles downwards as they mature.

'Red Sunset' is an early-flowering cultivar with attractive, soft orange flower heads.

Produced over a long period from late spring to mid-summer, these blooms will create a glorious massed display in coastal gardens, where salt winds are happily tolerated.

This is one of the hardier leucospermum species, withstanding exposed conditions and frost to −7°C. Well-drained soils and sunny planting positions are essential, as is the case with all leucospermums.

H: 3–4 m	Attracts birds
F: Spring–summer	Cut flowers
Frost-hardy	

Leucospermum reflexum var. 'luteum'

Cape gold

This exceptionally beautiful variety was discovered by South African botanists in the wild in 1973. It has since become widely cultivated in several countries, and in some is known simply as Cape gold. The flower heads are similar to the more common species *L. reflexum* in shape but are a lovely clear golden-yellow colour and

The appropriately named skyrocket pincushion.

are borne in profusion over the late spring and early summer months. They are used for commercial picking purposes in some countries.

L. reflexum var. 'luteum' has paler, more silver-green foliage than the species and is a less vigorous (usually not exceeding 2 m high) but still bushy shrub under cultivation.

This lovely leucospermum withstands wind (including salt-laden) well but tends to be a little more prone to frost damage than *L. reflexum*. Successful cultivation requires a sunny position with good drainage.

H: 2 m	Attracts birds
F: Spring–summer	Cut flowers
Medium frost-hardy	

Leucospermum 'Scarlet Ribbons'

A cross between *L. glabrum* and *L. tottum*, 'Scarlet Ribbons' is an excellent example of the potential that exists from this type of breeding, being colourful, vigorous and very free-flowering. It should not be confused with the Australian cultivar 'Ribbons', which is of *L. conocarpodendron* x *L. glabrum* origins and has yellow styles with red perianth 'ribbons'.

Forming a neat, dense bush of 1.5 x 1.5 m, this plant becomes smothered in its characteristic flower heads over late spring to midsummer. The pink styles contrast vividly with the rich red 'ribbons' of the flower perianth to give a bi-colour effect.

'Scarlet Ribbons' appreciates good drainage and a sunny position. It is hardier than many similar cultivars, withstanding frost and wind well, and will often produce flowers within a year of planting.

H: 1.5 m	Attracts birds
F: Spring–summer	Cut flowers
Medium frost-hardy	

Leucospermum 'Sunrise'

This colourful *L. cordifolium* x *L. patersonii* cultivar originating from the Fynbos Unit of the Vegetable and Ornamental Plant Institute of South Africa is a good example of the potential of this choice of parents for hybridising purposes.

The medium-sized orange-red flowers are produced in profusion about a month earlier than the *L. cordifolium* parent, and the depth of colour is especially

LEFT: The clear yellow flower heads of Cape gold can be seen for great distances when this variety is blooming.

ABOVE: 'Scarlet Ribbons' tumbles down a retaining wall, showing its versatility, not its usual habit of growth.

BELOW: Flower heads displaying the distinctive red 'ribbons' that gave rise to this cultivar's name.

'Sunrise' – a brilliantly coloured South African cultivar.

'Tango', a richly coloured recent release with long stems and a compact head, is an ideal cut flower.

noteworthy. Although not noted its for stem length unless pruned to promote this, 'Sunrise' does have excellent garden potential because of its early, colourful display, vigour and reliability. Home flower arrangers and floral artists will also find it appealing. It reaches to 2 m in height with a bushy habit and has attractive leaves, deeply notched at the tips.

'Sunrise' is tolerant of light frosts to –3 or –4°C, is usually wind-hardy, responds well to pruning and requires good drainage and a sunny position.

H: 2 m	Attracts birds
F: Spring–summer	Cut flowers
Tolerates light frosts	

Leucospermum 'Tango'

This recently released Hawaiian-raised cultivar of *L. glabrum* x *L. lineare* parentage displays vividly coloured heads of bloom, with bright red perianth ribbons contrasting strikingly with the orange styles. These flower heads are carried on exceptionally long stems that should provide excellent picking. They are produced relatively early in the season and carry on into the summer.

The bushes are dense and reach to about 2 m when mature. They are easily kept compact through picking or pruning. This appears to be a relatively hardy cultivar that will withstand midwinter temperatures of –4°C once thoroughly established. Good drainage is essential and a sunny position desirable to encourage flowering and maximum colour.

H: 2 m	Attracts birds
F: Spring–summer	Cut flowers
Medium frost-hardy	

Leucospermum 'Thompson's Gift'

This relatively recent introduction may become the most popular groundcover leucospermum for some years. A chance *L. conocarpodendron* x *L. hypophyllocarpodendron* hybrid discovered in South Africa's Cape Peninsula mountains, it was gifted to the Kirstenbosch National Botanic Gardens and has been distributed commercially from there.

Reaching to little more than 35 cm high with a spread of 1.5–2 m, 'Thompson's Gift' is an ideal subject for covering banks and will also form a vigorous mass of foliage and flowers to cascade over a wall. With regular pruning it may also have potential as a container plant.

'Thompson's Gift' is a handsome addition to the groundcover range of leucospermums.

The deep green leaves with their notched ends provide a perfect foil for the smaller brilliant clear yellow pincushion flowers, which are produced from spring to midsummer.

The main cultivation requirements for 'Thompson's Gift' are a well-drained, sunny and almost frost-free position. If these needs can be met, this should be an easy-to-grow proposition.

H: 35 cm x 1.5 m wide	Tolerates light frosts
F: Spring–summer	Attracts birds

Leucospermum tottum

In nature, this is a very variable species found growing in widely different habitats over a large area of South Africa's Cape. As a result, many forms are offered by nurseries. In New Zealand a selected form is marketed as 'Champagne', while in Australia another is sold as 'Tiny Tot'.

Generally this is a bushy, much-branched shrub of 1–1.5 m in both height and width. The open, somewhat spidery flower heads are a soft pink shade with

This selected form of *L. tottum* is sold as 'Champagne' in New Zealand and is typical of the more desirable variants found in the natural habitat.

mauve tips. As they age they deepen to assume a purplish hue. The main flowering time is from spring to midsummer. While not generally considered a cut-flower proposition, owing to its short stems, *L. tottum* in its various commercial forms is a very showy shrub.

This leucospermum is usually frost-tolerant to –3°C, requires a well-drained, sunny position in the garden and resents being crowded, preferring good air circulation to prevent fungal infection.

H: 1–1.5 m	Tolerates light frosts
F: Spring–summer	Attracts birds

Leucospermum 'Veldfire'

Appropriately named, 'Veldfire' has the appearance of a blazing fire, with the orange-red perianth 'ribbons' being the coals, and the golden-yellow styles the flames. A bush covered with the flower heads during mid-spring to early summer shows more red initially, but gradually yellow becomes dominant as the flowers age. This cultivar is a hybrid of *L. glabrum* parentage and has been marketed for the past 20 years. It is not regarded as a suitable commercial cut flower because the flower heads too readily snap off from the stems.

A colourful and compact bush, usually to about 1.5 m high, 'Veldfire' fits in neatly with smaller garden layouts. Its attractive deep green leaves have prominent 'teeth' tipped with red.

This is a relatively hardy cultivar, withstanding frosts of –5°C without difficulty, and is adaptable to varying soil types provided they are free-draining. Sunny positions are desirable to promote strong flower colour, and wind is not a major problem.

H: 1.5 m	Medium frost-hardy
F: Spring–summer	Attracts birds

'Veldfire' has both handsome foliage and flower heads, and is aptly named for its fiery colour combinations.

LOMATIA

A genus of nine or more species from Australia and at least three from South America, *Lomatia* may vary from a shrub of 1 m to trees that can reach 20 m in height. The immensely variable leaves are a feature of this genus, but in several cases, especially *L. ferruginea*, the flowers are conspicuous and very attractive.

Lomatia ferruginea

Although not widely cultivated, this beautifully symmetrical small tree has so many attractive features that it should be grown much more by gardeners over a broad climate range.

A Chilean species, it reaches 3 m or more in height and has particularly handsome fern-like foliage. Young growth and stems are covered with a rusty, velvety down, adding further to its appeal. The small yellow-and-red flowers are carried in spectacular clusters for a prolonged period during the summer months and are followed by intriguing little canoe-shaped seed pods. This species has been grown in a variety of situations and has proved popular in warmer parts of the United Kingdom. It can be used as a striking tub plant as well as a specimen tree for smaller gardens.

L. ferruginea is usually tolerant of midwinter temperature drops to –6°C, may be grown in full or filtered sun, and prefers good, well-drained soil in a sheltered position.

H: 3+ m	Medium frost-hardy
F: Summer	

An attractive Australian member of the genus, *Lomatia fraseri* attracts nectar-seeking birds.

Lomatia fraseri

Silky lomatia, forest lomatia, tree lomatia

This Australian species, found growing in New South Wales, Victoria and Tasmania, is particularly notable for its very variable leaves and its height. The foliage can range from entire leaves that may be regularly or irregularly toothed to pinnately lobed, with a number of intermediates, all of which may be found on a single bush. Height may vary from a shrub of 50 cm in

Lomatia ferruginea is a striking small tree that originates from South America.

125

exposed situations to a shrub of 2 m or even a tree of 7 m in sheltered positions.

Creamy-white flowers are produced in prominently displayed long racemes over summer and are attractive to nectar-seeking birds. The foliage is sometimes used for backing for floral arrangements.

Under cultivation, *Lomatia fraseri* is a fast-growing, slender shrub with arching branches. It is adaptable to both sun and semi-shade and, when established, is drought-resistant and frost-tolerant to about −6°C.

H: 2 m	Attracts birds
F: Summer	Cut foliage
Frost-hardy	

MACADAMIA

Apart from the many cultivars found in the commercial nut-growing industry, there are some seven species of *Macadamia* found in Australia (Queensland and northern New South Wales) and four in New Caledonia.

One of the tropical Australian species, *M. hildebrandii*, is also found in the Celebes. Because of the international significance of its nut production, *M. integrifolia* has been chosen for the species to be described here.

Macadamia integrifolia

Macadamia nut, Queensland nut, bauple nut

As well as in its native Australia, this world-renowned gourmet dessert nut tree is cultivated commercially in Hawaii, South Africa, New Zealand, Zimbabwe, Kenya, Malawi, California, Brazil, Costa Rica and Guatemala, and was recently established on China's Hainan Island. In Hawaii alone there are more than 4,000 hectares of plantings on the three main islands, which is surpassed only by the estimated 5,000 hectares in Australia. It is the most economically important species of the Proteaceae.

M. integrifolia is an erect, long-lived tree of up to 20 m that, in old age, can produce as much as 135 kg of nuts in a favourable season. The average crop from a 20-year-old tree is about 35 kg.

The ornamental pendant racemes of flowers can be

Both the flowers and nuts of the macadamia tree are appealing.

30 cm long and are a creamy-white colour. *M. tetraphylla* produces pink or purplish blooms. Both species flower in winter and spring. The coarse foliage is deep green and shiny. Young leaves are serrated and often a bronze-pink shade.

Macadamias are successfully cultivated in good, well-drained soils in sheltered positions where frost does not exceed more than –1 or –2°C.

H: To 20 m	Tolerates light frosts
F: Winter–spring	Edible nut crops

MIMETES

Regarded as perhaps the most spectacular genus of the protea family, the eleven species of *Mimetes* are endemic to the southern area of South Africa's Cape Province. They are characterised by distinctive flowers that nestle in the axils of the terminal leaves. These leaves are frequently brightly coloured and, with fifteen or more flower heads massed towards the tops of the stems, the effect can be quite spectacular.

The shrubs may vary from 1 to 6 m, though most are in the region of 1.5 m. One of the most beautiful species is *M. argenteus*, with its pink-and-mauve flowers reflecting in the shimmering silver-haired foliage. Unfortunately it is rarely seen in cultivation, so here the best-known and most easily grown species, *M. cucullatus*, is described.

Mimetes cucullatus

(previously *M. lyrigera*)

Common pagoda, red bottlebrush

This bushy shrub of up to 1.5 m responds well to pruning, having a rootstock from which shoots will arise. The bright red terminal leaf bracts have a rounded, hooded appearance and encase white-tufted flowers that are displayed throughout the year, especially in spring. Young leaf growth is also red and can be admired throughout the year in many districts.

A very colourful garden shrub, *M. cucullatus* is also highly regarded for picking purposes. It is ideally grown in a sunny position with reasonably good soil that is

H: 1.5 m	Medium frost-hardy
F: Year-round, especially spring	Cut flowers

moisture-retentive yet free-draining. Some summer watering is considered desirable in dry climates, as this plant is not drought-tolerant. It is, however, a good coastal garden subject.

Mimetes is an under-rated genus with a great future as a garden shrub. *M. cucullatus* is the best-known species.

PARANOMUS

Most of the eighteen species of *Paranomus* are found growing in the mountains of South Africa's Cape Province, but a few extend their habitat to sea level. Five of the species exhibit the unusual characteristic of having entire leaves on the flowering stems, while elsewhere on the bushes the leaves are finely divided. The species described here, *P. reflexus*, is by far both the best known and most widely cultivated. Very few of the other members of the genus have much horticultural potential to recommend them.

Paranomus reflexus

Van Staden's sceptre

This shrub is strong-growing and can form a dense shrub of 2 x 2 m. It has the unusual characteristic of having two distinct leaf types on the flowering stems. Most of the bush has fine, delicate-looking foliage, but as the flowering stem grows, the upper half develops broad entire leaves leaves below the flower spike. The spikes are bottlebrush-like, a greenish-yellow shade and may be 12 cm long. They are produced over winter on long stems, making them useful cut flowers.

P. reflexus is drought-tolerant once established and is easy to grow in most well-drained soils in sunny positions. Light frosts are tolerated, but temperatures below –3°C may damage flower buds. It responds well to pruning, which promotes a bushy habit.

H: 2 m	Tolerates light frosts
F: Winter	Cut flowers

Paranomus refexus is an intriguing member of the protea family, with foliage that changes shape on the flowering stems.

Persoonia pinifolia is appreciated by florists for its flowers, fruit and foliage.
It is also a highly ornamental garden shrub.

PERSOONIA

Persoonia is a large and complex Australian genus of some 54 species that has been extensively revised over the years. Most are commonly known in Australia as 'geebungs'. The former New Zealand member of the genus, *P. toru*, has been placed in a new genus of its own, *Toronia*.

Persoonia pinifolia

Pine leaf geebung

P. pinifolia, a native of coastal New South Wales, is perhaps the most attractive and best-known species of this genus. Its bright green needle-like foliage is carried on slightly weeping branches, and bright yellow flowers are conspicuously borne in drooping terminal racemes, 10 cm long, over summer and autumn. These are followed by dense clusters of purple fruit that weigh the branches down.

Used by florists for flowers, fruit and foliage, this shrub is tolerant of salt winds and medium frosts. Well-drained soil is necessary, and it will grow in sun or partial shade. It is notoriously difficult to propagate.

H: 2–3 m	Medium frost-hardy
F: Summer–autumn	Cut flowers and foliage

PROTEA

The best-known genus of the Proteaceae, and the one for which it is named, comprises some 136 species, the bulk of which are from the African continent, 82 proteas being found in South Africa alone (mainly in the Cape Floral Kingdom) and 35 in tropical Africa.

The incredible variation in flower size, foliage form and growth habit of this genus is characteristic of the entire family, and is in itself adequate justification for the use of the legendary Greek god Proteus' name by Linnaeus when he was classifying the family (see Introduction).

Ranging from procumbent species that spill over rocky outcrops in nature, through the more familiar bushy garden subjects, to small trees, the *Protea* genus also displays diversity in its foliage, ranging from small and needle-like to large and fleshy, as in the king proteas. Flowers may be quite tiny and even slightly perfumed, or small, cup-shaped and pendulous (as in *P. nana*) or even of dinner-plate dimensions. Some are pollinated by nectar-seeking birds; others, such as the ground-hugging proteas, by small rodents. Those native to mountainous environs are frost-hardy, while others from the mild, coastal regions are quite tender. Most cultivated proteas originate from South Africa's Cape Province and are classified as winter-rainfall species.

Those from the northern regions of South Africa, such as the Transvaal and Natal, are referred to as summer-rainfall species.

This is an intriguing genus, both horticulturally and botanically, with species that are being reclassified, rediscovered when thought extinct (see *P. holosericea*) and, occasionally, described for the first time. Some spectacular new hybrids developed in South Africa, Australia, New Zealand and Hawaii are being introduced into cultivation at an ever-increasing rate.

In South Africa, to help reduce the confusion caused by most members of the Proteaceae now being called 'proteas', this genus is being increasingly referred to by the old name 'sugarbush', and most species carry common names incorporating this.

Protea acaulos

Common ground sugarbush

P. acaulos is possibly one of the most forgiving and adaptable groundcover protea species for garden cultivation. It forms a dense, spreading prostrate plant with erectly held, attractive foliage to 15 cm high, and may form a tight mat 2 m wide. It spreads both by long trailing branches and underground stems, but is not invasive. Leaves of this species are variable, with two distinct forms being marketed: one has broad, rounded foliage, while the other has linear-shaped leaves and a more vigorous growth habit.

Flowers are generally at the ends of the branches (terminal) and are small and cup-shaped. Though variable in colour, most have green centres with the bracts flushed red on their outer surfaces. They are produced from spring into summer in most regions.

This species will grow and flower equally well in full sun or semi-shade, tolerates most reasonably well-drained soils and is frost-hardy to at least –6°C.

H: 15 cm	Frost-hardy
F: Spring–summer	

Protea acuminata

(previously *P. cedromontana*)

Cedarberg protea, black-rim sugarbush

It is difficult to understand why *P. acuminata* is not seen more often in cultivation, for it is an attractive and easily grown species.

LEFT: *Protea* 'Coleman's Hybrid' represents an excellent example of the hybridising potential of *P. magnifica*.

P. acaulos is one of the most reliable groundcover species.

Usually an open, fairly erect shrub of 1.5 m, occasionally more bushy, this protea has small, flat, linear, pointed leaves and dainty, 2.5–5 cm wide, cup-shaped flowers that are variable in colour. Sometimes a solid deep red, occasionally with the inner bract surfaces white, and in other cases red and green combined attractively together but usually with a fine black rim, they are borne during spring and early summer.

The dainty *P. acuminata* is variable in its colours.

A beautiful protea for posy work and similar floral uses, *P. acuminata* enjoys most sunny, well-drained situations and is tolerant of frosts to –6°C. It prefers dry conditions and can be subject to fungal problems in humid climates.

H: 1.5 m	Frost-hardy
F: Spring	Cut flowers

Protea amplexicaulis

Stem-clasped protea, ivy-leafed protea, clasping-leaf sugarbush

This fascinating plant, which bears leaves strongly resembling some *Eucalyptus* species, is unlike any other protea in both its foliage and very distinctive flower heads.

With its low, sprawling habit (1.5 x 1.5 m), *P. amplexicaulis* is ideally suited to banks and walls, where its dense, cascading character can be displayed to full advantage. It provides a unique landscape feature with its thick, succulent, heart-shaped blue-green leaves. Young growth has a vivid pink colour, especially in winter. Also at this time of year the wide-open cup-shaped flowers can be found nestling on their minimal stems among the foliage. These are a deep purplish brown on the outside of the bracts, and white on the inner surface. The domed central floral mass is predominantly red.

The extraordinary leaves of *P. amplexicaulis* could convince the uninitiated that this plant is a eucalypt.

A frost-hardy and wind-tolerant species, this protea is a suitable subject for cold-climate gardens and is less successful in warm, humid regions. Good drainage is necessary, and either full or filtered sun is acceptable to this very appealing plant.

H: 30 cm x 1.5 m wide	Frost-hardy
F: Winter	

Protea aristata

Small pine sugarbush, Ladismith protea, Ladismith sugarbush

A neat, erect, slow-growing bush of 1.5–2 m high, this distinctive protea has unusual pine-needle-like foliage and produces 14 cm long flower heads of bright crimson with a silvery 'bloom' that softens the effect. These appear on long stems during late summer.

Distinctive rich green narrow foliage provides a lovely background to the striking flower heads of *P. aristata*.

Usually a long-lived and handsome garden subject, *P. aristata* has a free-flowering habit when few other proteas are on display. However, its unpleasantly pungent foliage may restrict its use for cut-flower purposes. Stripping foliage that will be under water in flower arrangements can reduce the problem.

RIGHT: *P. aristata* provides welcome late-summer flowers.

Dry climates are preferred by this surprisingly frost-tolerant (to −7°C) species. Warm, humid conditions can encourage fungal diseases that may lead to its demise.

H: 1.5–2 m	Attracts birds
F: Late summer	Cut flowers
Frost-hardy	

Protea aurea

(previously *P. longiflora*)

Shuttlecock protea, common shuttlecock sugarbush, potberg sugarbush (*P. aurea* subsp. *potbergensis*)

A well-known hardy species that has been cultivated by gardeners in several countries for probably a hundred years, *P. aurea* (best known to older gardeners by its former name of *P. longiflora*) has been used in hybridising and is still available from specialist nurseries.

Characterised by the 'shuttlecock' flowers, which range in colour from creamy white through pale pinks to a deep pinkish red, this species is particularly colourful from late summer through autumn into winter. *P. aurea* forms a tall (to 3 m), bushy shrub with an obvious trunk. It has variable foliage, with some forms having leathery, shiny leaves, while those on others are softer and hairy.

Although very attractive, this protea is not usually regarded as a cut-flower subject, but when picked at the soft bud stage it will gradually open in the vase and

P. aurea is a very variable species, displaying numerous flower colours from white through pink shades to red.

give a vase life of up to a week before the long styles collapse. It is one of the more hardy species, tolerating temperatures to −7°C, and is easily grown and long-lived in most well-drained, sunny situations.

| H: 3 m | Frost-hardy |
| F: Summer–winter | Attracts birds |

A deep reddish-pink form of *P. aurea*, 'Goodwood Red', is sold in New Zealand, where its hardiness is popular in colder areas.

Protea caffra 'White Ruby'

This interesting Australian selection is reputed to be of hybrid origins and is an erect-growing shrub to 3 m high with a spread of 1.5 m.

The large flower heads have a soft red colouring on the outer surfaces and tips of the bracts, a pure white on the inside, and the central flower mass is creamy white tipped with a rusty-bronze shade. Blooms are produced over several months during winter and spring, are appealing to nectar-seeking birds and have excellent vase life when picked. Heavy picking or pruning after flowering will help keep this cultivar bushy and compact. Neglect will tend to see it become somewhat 'leggy' in appearance.

Once established, 'White Ruby' is drought-resistant and will tolerate frost to –4°C. A sunny position with free-draining soil is desirable.

H: 3 m	Attracts birds
F: Winter–spring	Cut flowers
Medium frost-hardy	

'White Ruby', a *P. caffra* selection, is popular in Australia.

Protea 'Candy'

One of the many outstanding cultivars originating from Proteaflora, the largest Australian wholesale protea nursery, 'Candy' is an excellent example of the characteristics imparted to its hybrid progeny by *Protea longifolia*, the dominant parent.

'Candy', a recent hybrid introduction with *P. longifolia* parentage, offers a delightful mix of colours in its flower heads.

The long narrow leaves with slightly waved margins are typical of this parent plant, as are many of the flower features, such as the prominent peaked flower mass with its deep wine-coloured tip and the elongated shape of the head. The bracts, too, reveal the parentage, as they have minimal overlap towards their ends, showing the central flower mass through the gaps. The flowers have good stem length and are anticipated to have good cut-flower potential.

The bush is vigorous, reaching to 2 m high, and will tolerate wind and a range of soil types, but is susceptible to frosts below about –2°C.

H: 2 m	Attracts birds
F: Winter–spring	Cut flowers
Tolerates light frosts	

'Christine', a lovely hybrid of *P. compacta* parentage, displays its clear pink buds edged with silvery-white hairs.

Protea 'Christine'

This beautiful Australian cultivar is a hybrid of *Protea compacta* parentage and exhibits the clean-coloured floral bracts typical of that species. However, because 'Christine' displays more influence of the *P. compacta* parentage than do many others of this type of hybrid, it is difficult to pinpoint the other likely parent plant.

Flowering is at a useful time over autumn and early winter. Rich pink bracts with silvery-white highlights surround a similarly coloured peaked centre. The heads are slim and compact, and the stems are long, contributing to the usefulness of this cultivar as a commercial cut-flower proposition. Being very free-flowering and showy, it is also ideal for a larger home garden or as a specimen feature in a smaller-sized plot. Pruning will assist in keeping it to more manageable proportions for tight situations.

The bush will mature to a height of 2.5 m and a spread of some 2 m. It should be drought-resistant and frost-hardy to –4°C when established, and will usually adapt well to most well-drained soils in both coastal and inland districts.

H: 2.5 m	Attracts birds
F: Autumn–winter	Cut flowers
Medium frost-hardy	

Protea 'Clark's Red'

In 1948 the first New Zealand-raised protea cultivar was created when the breeder observed a tui, a native nectar-seeking bird, working flowers of neighbouring *Protea aurea* and *P. repens* bushes and saved the seed of this cross. The resultant natural hybrid has become a stock-in-trade of many nurseries and, while its attributes have been surpassed by most other protea cultivars, it is still widely grown and sold throughout New Zealand by garden centres.

The popularity of this protea is due to three main features: it flowers virtually year-round; it is remarkably frost-hardy; and its very deep red colour combines with the silvery tips to the styles to produce a distinctively coloured flower. Although it is notorious for the leaf tips blackening with a fungus problem, especially in humid, sheltered environs, most gardeners tolerate this fault for the plant's other features.

Forming a dense, erect bush of up to 2.5 m, 'Clark's Red' will withstand frosts of up to –12°C, is adaptable to most soils and will perform well in both full sun and semi-shade. It is not noted for pickability but is much

'Clark's Red' – a popular New Zealand-raised cultivar.

loved by nectar-seeking birds and is a reliable, long-lived garden shrub.

H: 2.5 m	Frost-hardy
F: Year-round	Attracts birds

Protea compacta

Bot River protea, Bot River sugarbush, prince protea

P. compacta is a very well-known species in its native South Africa, and a significant number of cultivars have been derived from it and are becoming established as garden plants and cut-flower subjects in other countries. The natural vigour, clean bract colour and long stems are sought-after characteristics that are readily imparted to its hybrid progeny. Two Australian-raised examples are 'Christine' and 'Pink Princess', while 'Franciscan Hybrid' is a New Zealand hybrid.

In cultivation this protea forms a tall open bush to 3.5 m unless kept well pruned from an early age to create a well-branched framework. Thick, fleshy leaves are a characteristic of the species. The neat flower heads, which can vary from pure white through soft pink to almost red, are carried on long, stout stems over much of the year, but especially in winter. Although not noted for good vase life, this species has been picked in the wild in the Cape for many decades.

Easily grown in most well-drained soils in sunny positions, *P. compacta* is wind-tolerant, but buds can be damaged by frosts harsher than –4°C.

H: 3.5 m	Medium frost-hardy
F: Year-round, especially	Attracts birds
winter	Cut flowers

Protea 'Coleman's Hybrid'

A very appealing cultivar, 'Coleman's Hybrid' originated in New Zealand during the late 1970s from imported *P. magnifica* seed. The other parent may be *P. compacta*. Not always available in the trade in New Zealand because of propagating difficulties, it nevertheless is widely grown by enthusiastic gardeners.

Of dense, erect growth habit to 2 m or slightly more, this vigorous cultivar has the typical glaucous leathery foliage of *P. magnifica* but the flower heads differ markedly. These are a rich silvery-pink colouring, more elongated than *P. magnifica* and have spectacular pure white beards to the tips of the bracts. The central flower mass is a clear white and is especially symmetrical in its form. The flowers are produced from spring into

P. compacta is variable in both flower form and colour.

'Coleman's Hybrid' – an attractive protea that flowers for months on end.

The bright apple-green bracts of *Protea coronata* always attract attention.

summer, and even autumn in some localities. Its good vase life and long sturdy stems make this protea an excellent picking subject.

Frost-hardy to –4°C once well established, 'Coleman's Hybrid' is long-lived and generally wind-tolerant. It prefers well-drained soils and sunny positions, and will respond to light pruning after flowering.

H: 2 m	Attracts birds
F: Spring	Cut flowers
Medium frost-hardy	

Protea coronata

(previously *P. macrocephala* and *P. incompta*)

Apple-green protea, green sugarbush

P. coronata produces unusual flower heads of bright Granny Smith apple green that are characterised by the incurved bracts surrounding the white-tufted (sometimes red) flowers. These are freely produced for months on end during winter and spring, and have some cut-flower potential.

A tall, dense shrub of up to 3 m, this species forms a heavy trunk and is long-lived. It responds well to pruning, which will keep it to a more manageable size in the smaller garden. The soft, slightly hairy leaves are another feature of the shrub, but these can be damaged by frosts below –2°C.

This is a suitable plant for coastal gardens, withstanding salt winds well, and is noted for being one of just a handful of proteas that are tolerant of alkaline soils.

H: 3 m	Attracts birds
F: Winter–spring	Cut flowers
Tolerates light frosts	

Protea cynaroides

King protea, king sugarbush

The most spectacular and largest-flowered protea is also the national flower of South Africa and the best-known member of the family. Some 80 naturally occurring variants of *P. cynaroides* have been described, and these are divided into groups mainly according to leaf type. The glabrous leaves vary from large and rounded to small and narrow, and the huge flowers can be very wide open or narrowly funnel-shaped and can range from a

RIGHT: This lovely white-flowered form of *P. cynaroides* is marketed as 'Arctic Ice'.

There are many variants of *Protea cynaroides*, the king protea.

pure greenish white through soft silvery pinks to deep red. Each of these variants has its own distinct flowering time. Additionally, in Australia two dwarf variants are being marketed as 'Mini Kings' and suitable for tub culture.

In general terms, selected king proteas under cultivation are broad, bushy shrubs, up to 2 m high with a similar spread. The colours are typically either the soft silvery pinks or deeper pinkish-red tones. Good white selections are now also available. Spring- and early summer-flowering types seem to be the most popular. The largest selections may be almost as big as dinner plates, but bread-and-butter-plate dimensions are the norm.

Because *P. cynaroides* has an underground rootstock from which it can shoot into new growth after veld fires, it can be rigorously pruned back to a stump if it becomes 'leggy' in old age or is damaged. The vigorous new growth is almost akin to regeneration. Some forms are able to withstand frosts of −6°C or more; others are less hardy. Most seem tolerant of coastal conditions but all appreciate some summer moisture. The king protea is an adaptable shrub in most sunny, well-drained garden situations, and in nature is noted for its ability to grow in acid soils with pH levels as low as 3.5.

H: 2 m	Attracts birds
F: Variable	Cut flowers
Medium frost-hardy	

Protea eximea

(previously *P. latifolia*)

Ray-flowered protea, broad-leaf sugarbush, duchess protea

The duchess protea was popular with gardeners in some countries during the 1950s and 1960s, when choice was limited, and it became known as a hardy and reliable larger shrub suitable for garden display but not for picking purposes. Improved forms, with brighter colours and better form, have kept its popularity alive.

Usually a large, open shrub of up to 3 m, *P. eximea* can vary markedly in habit. While summer is the usual time for flowering, some variants bloom throughout the year. The large, colourful flower heads have spoon-shaped bracts of red with the tips of the central flower mass displaying the typical purplish wine-coloured awns. Selected forms such as 'Duchess of Perth' are particularly colourful. Leaves are quite broad, grey-green and often have a purple tinge.

This is normally a hardy species that can withstand harsh winters. It is also adaptable to a variety of well-drained soils and is drought-resistant once established.

H: 3 m	Attracts birds
F: Mainly summer	Frost-hardy

'Duchess of Perth', a selected form of *Protea eximea*.

Protea 'Franciscan Hybrid'

A New Zealand-raised cultivar presumed to be a natural hybrid of *P. compacta* and *P. magnifica* originating from imported seed, this attractive long-lived shrub matures to a densely broad specimen of 2.5 m high by 3 m wide.

The large, clear pink flower heads are overlaid with a fine silvery pubescence and the central dome is a deep wine-red colour. These are carried in profusion over spring, with a few blooms also produced in autumn. They have long stems and are suitable for picking.

141

The large-flowered 'Franciscan Hybrid' will adapt to a range of soil types.

Moderately hardy, 'Franciscan Hybrid' may have its buds and young foliage damaged by frosts greater than −4°C. It adapts to heavier clay soils, flowers more prolifically in open, sunny positions, and tolerates wind.

H: 2.5 m	Attracts birds
F: mainly spring	Cut flowers
Medium frost-hardy	

Protea 'Frosted Fire'

A particularly floriferous cultivar, 'Frosted Fire' produces masses of brilliant flowers that are well displayed above the foliage. These are carried on medium-length stems over winter and spring, are a rich red colour lightly tipped with silver, and have a wine centre. They are not often used for commercial picking purposes but are beautiful for home arrangements and may be successfully dried.This is a good example of some of the outstanding hybrids that are beginning to be brought into cultivation. It is of *P. neriifolia* parentage, together with either *P. compacta* or, more likely, *P. longifolia.*

A colourful and popular garden subject, 'Frosted Fire' is generally a compact, bushy shrub reaching a height of little more than 1.5 m, but in some gardens will reach

'Frosted Fire' flowers prolifically from a young age.

Rich red flower bracts tipped with silver-white hair are a feature of 'Frosted Fire'.

drained, sunny gardens, where it will prove a magnificent, long-lived specimen. It is wind-tolerant and will survive frosts as low as –7°C.

H: 2 m	Attracts birds
F: Summer	Cut flowers
Frost-hardy	

The beautiful *Protea grandiceps* has intriguing variants, both in size and colouring.

2.5 m. Pruning after flowering from the first season will help to keep shrubs compact. Reasonably frost-tolerant to at least –3°C, once established this protea is easily grown in most well-drained, sunny positions.

H: 1.5–2.5 m	Attracts birds
F: Winter–spring	Cut flowers
Medium frost-hardy	

Protea grandiceps

Peach protea, princess protea, red sugarbush

Both the leaves and flower heads of *Protea grandiceps* are very distinctive. This is a dense bush, growing to 2 m high with a greater spread. The lush deep green leaves are glaucous and leathery, and have red margins.

The large flower heads are encased by the leaves and have incurved bracts of rich peach-red or coral. These are heavily tipped with luxuriant, feathery tips of white or purplish brown and surround the creamy-white flower mass, which is never fully displayed. Very stout stems are necessary to support the weight of this heavy head during the flowering time of late spring to mid-summer, depending on locality.

This handsome protea is easily grown in most well-

Protea holosericea

Saw-edge sugarbush

One of the rarest proteas as well as one of the loveliest, this species was believed to be extinct for 164 years from 1801 until rediscovery in 1965, and only a few hundred individual plants exist in nature. Fortunately it is in cultivation in South Africa, Australia and New Zealand. It is slow to propagate, however, so will always be in short supply.

Usually forming a low, spreading bush of 1.3 m tall and 2 m wide, this slow-growing protea superficially resembles a small *P. magnifica*, but the flowers are quite different and exceptionally beautiful, with predominantly white bracts that are heavily tipped with black fur. The central cream floral mass has a prominent black peak, adding further to the striking black-and-white pattern. These are normally produced during the mid-spring months, but in some climates can be seen over late winter.

The blooms are carried on short horizontal stems, often with a semi-pendulous habit. They make delightfully different, long-lasting cut flowers and also dry particularly well.

The exquisite *Protea holosericea*. INSET: A dried flower head keeps remarkable colour after ten years.

P. holosericea's rocky habitat, with snowy winters and harsh dry summers, is indicative of its preferred conditions. Frost is not usually a problem, but full sun is preferred. Rich soils and fertilisers are to be avoided, as are moist, humid climates.

| H: 1.3 m x 2 m wide | Attracts birds |
| F: Mainly spring | Frost-hardy |

Protea 'Joey'

This extraordinary cultivar serves to demonstrate just how much potential exists for hybridisation between protea species. Originating from a seedling *P. amplexicaulis*, the other parent possibly being *P. venusta*, 'Joey' is an Australian-raised cultivar of unique appearance that forms a plant of 1 m or less in height with a spread of 2 m or more. It has great potential as a taller groundcover or for covering a bank, and also has considerable curiosity value.

The hanging flower heads are cup-shaped and 80 mm or more across. The predominantly bright scarlet-red colour on the outer surfaces of the bracts shades to cream at the base and a shining creamy white on the inner surfaces. They are produced freely over winter to early spring and are reputed to be suitable for picking and also for drying.

An unlikely hybrid, Protea 'Joey' is a startling new cultivar.

'Joey' can be grown in a range of free-draining soils, will flower more freely in sunny positions, and tolerate frost to −5°C. Once established, it should withstand drought conditions well.

H: 1 m	Attracts birds
F: Winter	Cut flowers
Medium frost-hardy	

Protea 'Kurrajong Rose'

This Australian-raised cultivar is another example of the incredible potential that exists for hybridising between the protea species. While it has only been sold in limited numbers to date in Australia and New Zealand, it has definite 'marketability'.

'Kurrajong Rose' combines the clear, slightly waxen bracts of *P. burchellii* with the size and foliage of *P. magnifica* to create a very distinctive flower head exhibiting some of the best features of both parent plants. These appealing blooms appear from midwinter to spring on a compact, bushy shrub of 1.5 m high.

As with so many hybrids, this protea has good vigour and, with the influence of the *P. burchellii* parent, is adaptable to a broad range of soil types provided they drain freely. It is drought-resistant once established and is hardy to about −5°C in most areas.

A *P. magnifica* x *P. burchellii* cultivar, 'Kurrajong Rose' is appealing for its clear colouring.

H: 1.5 m	Attracts birds
F: Winter–spring	Cut flowers
Medium frost-hardy	

Protea laevis

Although a comparative rarity in cultivation, the lovely broad-leaved forms of this low-growing species should be considered by nurserymen and gardeners alike. It cannot quickly be reproduced from cuttings but does germinate freely from viable seed.

This is a very variable protea in nature, with growth habit and foliage displaying considerable differences. The outstanding form illustrated has a dense, ground-hugging habit to 1 m wide. It has broad, glaucous, erectly held foliage and well-displayed large flowers that have pale greenish-cream bracts flushed with a soft carmine at the base. These are produced during early spring to summer, according to locality, and are particularly eye-catching.

Protea laevis is a rare and lovely low-growing species.

P. laevis is a notably frost-hardy species, coming as it does from mountainous regions of the Cape, and also withstands summer droughts. It is adaptable to varying soil types, and in cooler climates appears to be long-lived, flowering consistently every spring.

H: 30 cm x 1 m wide	Frost-hardy
F: Spring–summer	

Protea laurifolia

Grey-leaf sugarbush

In nature this is a very widespread and common protea. It is a hardy, easily grown species and is often mistaken for *P. neriifolia*, but can be normally be distinguished by its broad grey-green foliage. It is also a more vigorous and longer-lived plant.

P. laurifolia attains a height of up to 3 m, with a stout trunk and a neat, erect growth habit, but may be kept pruned as a smaller shrub. It can live to 30 years or more under cultivation and is noted for its reliability and trouble-free character.

The flower heads are variable in colour, ranging from greenish white with purplish beards to pale peach or deep pinkish red with black beards. While most forms are desirable garden plants, they have not been exploited as commercial cut flowers, perhaps because they have a slightly shorter stem length than some other species. However, they usually do pick well and are sometimes used by floral artists to good effect.

This hardy and adaptable plant withstands heavy frost, wind and a wide range of soil types. It prefers sunny positions if it is to flower well, and is regarded as an 'easy' protea under cultivation.

H: 3 m	Frost-hardy
F: Year-round, especially	Attracts birds
winter–spring	Cut flowers

'Peach Sheen', a large-flowered example of *P. laurifolia*.

The unusual colourings of *Protea laurifolia* 'Royal Crest' create interest.

'Rose Mink' is a hardy *P. laurifolia* cultivar that flowers year round.

Protea lepidocarpodendron

Black protea, black-beard sugarbush, black mink

Gardeners find this species somewhat controversial, black being a colour that has an association with death for some, while others delight in the thick purplish-black velvety fur that so heavily tips the white or occasionally pale pink bracts. These slim flower heads, superficially similar to *P. neriifolia* in shape, are borne over a long period during winter and are occasionally used for picking purposes, although the bush is more often grown as a curiosity by collectors.

P. lepidocarpodendron is a fast-growing, dense bush, to 2.5 m high, and will need to be regularly pruned if a compact habit is to be retained. It should ideally be replaced as a garden plant every 10–12 years when it begins to become 'leggy'.

This species is a good coastal subject, withstanding salt winds well, but it will not survive frosts below −1 or −2°C. It prefers reasonably moist, humid conditions, and attempting to grow it in hot dry climates will lead to disappointment.

H: 2.5 m	Attracts birds
F: Winter	Cut flowers
Tolerates light frosts	

P. lepidocarpodendron, the extraordinary black protea.

147

Protea lorifolia

Strap-leaf sugarbush

While not widely cultivated, *P. lorifolia* is common in the wild and is conspicuous because of its very large leathery grey-green leaves, which are hairy when young. Although the short-stemmed flower heads are not small compared with other proteas, they are dwarfed by the surrounding foliage. However, the mainly pink-and-cream blooms are quite well displayed during autumn and early winter. A number of forms occur in nature, displaying variations in flower shape and colour in particular.

Although ultimately reaching a height of 2.5 m, this protea is relatively slow-growing and for some years may be broad bush of little more than 1 m high. At this stage the blooms are more readily seen and the bush is therefore more attractive. To some extent, pruning may keep it at this stage for several years.

P. lorifolia is something of a collector's item, but its adaptability to climates with cold winters and dry summers, plus its spectacular foliage, combine to make it worthy of consideration by gardeners.

H: 2.5 m	Frost-hardy
F: Autumn–winter	

Protea magnifica

(previously *P. barbigera*)

Queen protea, bearded protea, woolly-headed protea, giant woolly-beard

Second only to the massive king protea (*P. cynaroides*) in size, *P. magnifica* is aptly named, for its huge woolly-bearded blooms create an arresting sight. Coming from mountainous regions of South Africa's Cape at altitudes of up to 2,700 m, this hardy species will withstand cold in winter and dry, hot spells over summer. In cultivation it is adaptable to a range of well-drained soils and thrives in most temperate climates.

The queen protea forms a large, dense bush of 2 x 2 m or more and has large leathery leaves, hairy when young and usually blue-green and glabrous with maturity. The spectacular woolly flower heads may measure up to 15 cm wide with an equal or greater length. Some variants of *P. magnifica* have smaller, semi-pendulous flowers, but the larger, erectly held examples are most popular with gardeners and flower growers. Colour is extremely variable, ranging from creamy white through soft silvery pinks to rosy reds. The central flower mass often has a black peak, which is variable in size, but other examples have pure creamy-white centres.

The huge leaves of *P. lorifolia* almost overpower the flower heads.

ABOVE and RIGHT: The appropriately named *P. magnifica* is infinitely variable.

Flowering time is also variable, commencing in mid-winter with some variants and going through to early summer with others.

A wide range of colour forms and hybrid cultivars are being developed for commercial flower growers and home gardeners.

H: 2+ m	Attracts birds
F: Mainly spring	Cut flowers
Frost-hardy	

Protea 'May Day'

One of the many *P. magnifica* x *P. neriifolia* cultivars now being marketed by nurseries, this attractive protea produces large flower heads that bear more resemblance to *P. magnifica* than the other parent, although its influence can be seen. Large blooms are produced over an extended period from late winter through spring, and the pinkish-red bracts are trimmed with silvery-white fur and tufts of black. The central flower dome is a rich wine-red colour, providing a pleasing contrast.

In some regions the growth of this cultivar rarely exceeds 1 x 1 m, but where growth is encouraged by

The large-flowered 'May Day' is compact in habit.

mild temperatures it may reach 2.5m in height. A vigorous plant, it has a very free-flowering habit and the stems are suitable for picking.

'May Day' tolerates wind and is usually frost-hardy to –4°C. It requires free-draining soils and will flower more enthusiastically in sunny positions.

H: 1–2.5 m	Attracts birds
F: Winter–spring	Cut flowers
Medium frost-hardy	

Protea nana

(previously *P. roseaceae*)

Mountain rose, mountain rose sugarbush

The delightful little mountain rose is so unlike most of the better-known protea species that it often confounds the average gardener.

Growing to just a metre tall, this densely branched shrub is covered with rich green needle-like leaves and produces masses of small, bell-shaped hanging blooms during winter and spring. Wine-red bracts surround a buff-coloured central flower mass, which deepens in

The gorgeous little mountain rose hangs its head.

colour towards its peak. They are often seen at their best when looking from below at shrubs planted on a bank.

Not always easily grown, *P. nana* seems to prefer heavier soils with more moisture than many proteas. It is surprisingly hardy and may be grown in either sun or partial shade, the latter not affecting flowering.

| H: 1 m | Frost-hardy |
| F: Winter–spring | Cut flowers (posies) |

Protea neriifolia

Oleander-leaved protea, narrow-leaf sugarbush, 'Pink Mink'

Protea neriifolia probably ranks as the most widely cultivated protea outside its native South Africa. It has the distinction of being the first protea formally described by botanists in 1605 and was cultivated in conservatories in England and Europe during the early 1800s. It was offered by at least two nurseries during the mid-1930s in New Zealand, where it became the most well-known protea in cultivation until relatively recently, when newer cultivars have competed for popularity.

Usually this is a dense shrub of up to 3 m in height with bright green oleander-like leaves. The flower heads, while always similar in shape, vary greatly in colour. The bracts can range from pure white through soft greens and pinks to deep reds, with beards varying from white to black. The central flower dome can also vary from cream shades through buff to wine in the case of some cultivars. The flowering period is very prolonged, with some flowering almost year-round, but they are mainly seen during autumn to spring with a peak over winter. There are innumerable cultivars of this protea marketed by nurseries, and most are outstanding plants for both garden display and picking purposes. These include 'Alba', 'Big Mink', 'Chunn's White', 'Cream Mink', 'Feathered Red', 'Green Ice', 'Green Velvet', 'Lett's White', 'Limelight', 'Margaret Watling', 'Pink Mink', 'Purity', 'Ruby', 'Silk 'n' Satin', 'Silvertips' and 'Snowcrest'. Unfortunately, only a few can be illustrated here.

Although in nature *P. neriifolia* grows in light, sandy soils and mild, moist climates, under cultivation it has proved to be one of the most adaptable proteas, thriving in a wide range of soils provided they drain freely.

H: 2–3 m	Attracts birds
F: Autumn–spring	Cut flowers
Medium frost-hardy	

Protea neriifolia 'Green Ice'.

Protea neriifolia 'Silver Tips'.

Protea neriifolia 'Margaret Watling'.

Protea neriifolia 'Ruby'.

Protea nitida

(previously *P. arborea*)

Waboom, wagon tree

This intriguing species of either small tree proportions (to 7 m) or a dwarf, multi-trunked growth habit has been in limited cultivation in a number of countries for many years. Its popularity with connoisseurs and collectors is probably due to the massive gnarled trunk that develops with age in the case of tree forms, the large silvery-green glaucous leaves and the striking pink-to-red young growth.

In the early days of settlement in South Africa's Cape, timber of this species was used for a variety of purposes including construction of wagons, furniture and flooring.

The green 'shaving brush' flowers are highly distinctive, neat when first opening, but the silvery flower mass quickly collapses inwards in an untidy fashion. The bracts are usually green, occasionally pink, and are attractive, especially at the bud stage. The blooms are prominently displayed, especially over late winter and spring, with an occasional flowering in other seasons.

P. nitida is a long-lived species, often attaining an age of a hundred years. An easily grown protea, it thrives in a range of well-drained soils, in sun or semi-shade, and tolerates frost to at least −5°C.

H: Tree to 7 m	F: Winter–spring
Shrub to 1 m	Medium frost-hardy

LEFT: *Protea neriifolia* 'Purity'.

Protea nitida – the famous waboom.

Protea obtusifolia

'Red Baron', limestone sugarbush

This protea has been cultivated in Europe since the mid-nineteenth century and elsewhere since the early twentieth. Not only are the well-displayed flower heads appealing for their clear, waxen bracts of either bright red or greenish ivory, but the bush itself is very tolerant of coastal salt-laden winds and, unlike most protea, alkaline soils with pH levels up to 8.4.

Under cultivation *P. obtusifolia* is a well-shaped shrub up to 3 m high, and is regarded as both long-lived and reliable. Provided some pruning is carried out from the early stages to ensure a good framework of lower

Like many proteas, *P. obtusifolia* is very variable in colour.

branches, it should retain a neat shape well into old age. The tidy glabrous flowers usually have bright scarlet-red bracts that tightly overlap. Pinkish-red and pure white forms also occur. Although they do make excellent cut flowers, a limited stem length restricts their use by florists. The main flowering period is over late autumn and early winter, but heads can be seen through to early spring.

Early frosts can cause damage to buds and soft growth, and −2°C is possibly the coldest frost this species will endure without conspicuous damage.

H: 3 m	Attracts birds
F: Autumn–winter	Cut flowers
Tolerates light frosts	

Protea 'Pink Ice'

(previously *Protea* 'Silvan Pink')

'Pink Ice' has become the biggest-selling protea cultivar in Australia and New Zealand over the past decade, both to home gardeners and commercial flower growers. It is fast-growing and reliable, flowers virtually year-round and has particularly appealing flowers produced on long stems that are very suitable for picking purposes. A similar cultivar, 'Special Pink Ice', with more brightly coloured flowers has been recently introduced in Australia.

This Australian hybrid is probably of *P. compacta* x *P. susannae* origins, although it has been suggested that *P. neriifolia* may be a possible parent. It forms a dense, upright bush to 3 x 3 m within 10 years, although careful pruning, keeping within leaf growth, will keep it to more manageable proportions. The beautiful heads of bloom are a clear, rich silvery pink, with no beard, and the central flower dome is a buff colour with a wine-tinted peak. Flowers are carried terminally and are well displayed against the neat, dense foliage of mid-green colouring. The overall effect provides for a very handsome bush. Autumn, winter and spring are the peak flowering periods, with a few blooms produced over summer.

Adaptable to a variety of well-drained soil types, this easily grown protea withstands winds and coastal conditions well and is frost-tolerant to about −5°C in most districts.

H: 3 m	Medium frost-hardy
F: Year round, especially	Attracts birds
autumn–spring	Cut flowers

Protea 'Pink Princess'

'Pink Princess' is a spectacular cultivar that originated from the Proteaflora Nursery in Australia and reaffirms the significance of *Protea compacta* as a parent plant in this type of hybrid protea. The richly coloured clean bracts are typical of the characteristics inherited in this cross. Although the other parent plant is not specified, it is almost certainly *P. magnifica*, as suggested by the very large leathery leaves and the hairiness of the floral bracts.

The large, handsome flower heads are a particularly deep clear pink with silvery-white hairs edging the bracts. The central flower mass is a combination of deep pink and silvery white, adding further to the overall appearance. These blooms are produced during the winter and spring months and are carried on long stems with handsome foliage, making them suitable as cut flowers.

Growing to a large bush of 2.5 m high x 1.5 m wide, this is a moderately frost-hardy (to about –4°C) protea that is reported to be adaptable to a range of conditions,

'Pink Princess', an Australian-raised cultivar, has large flower heads of an especially rich pink colouring.

both coastal and inland, provided free-draining soils and sunny positions are provided. Once established, it should be drought-tolerant.

H: 2.5 m	Attracts birds
F: Winter–spring	Cut flowers
Medium frost-hardy	

Protea 'Possum Magic'

An unusual Australian-raised cultivar of *P. magnifica* x *P. longifolia* origins, this particularly distinctive protea is likely to become established as a firm favourite with gardeners. The medium-to-large flower heads are produced over the spring months and are slightly waxen in appearance, with more *P. longifolia* influence and lacking the woolly beards of *P. magnifica*. The floral bracts are handsomely flushed and tipped with bright orange-bronze, shading to cream at their base. The

'Pink Ice' is one of the most popular protea cultivars.

155

central peaked flower dome is heavily tipped with black, providing a strong contrast.

The leaves of this dense, 2 m high x 1.5 m wide bush are a rich blue-green, strongly reminiscent of the *P. magnifica* parent, and are an attractive feature of the shrub when not in flower.

'Possum Magic' is very suitable for using as a colourful specimen bush in the garden and has excellent picking potential. It should prove hardy to occasional winter frosts of –4°C, prefers well-drained, sunny positions, and is usually wind-tolerant and drought-resistant.

H: 2 m	Attracts birds
F: Spring	Cut flowers
Medium frost-hardy	

'Possum Magic' is a lovely Australian-raised protea hybrid.

Protea 'Profusion'

Although this cultivar is not readily available, it has been included here because of the significance of the breeding involved. 'Profusion' is a *P. pudens* x *P. neriifolia* cultivar that has been marketed in relatively small numbers over the years in New Zealand. It is the *P. pudens* parentage that is interesting because of the smaller flowers and neat growth produced with this cross, making it ideal for the home garden. In Australia a *P. pudens* x *P. longifolia* cultivar named 'Pixie', of similarly compact habit, is marketed. There are many other *P. pudens* hybrid seedlings in private collections that have not been exploited, some with delightful smaller flowers and very compact growth habits, giving them commercial potential.

'Profusion' produces large numbers of neat flowers, with rich pink bracts delicately fringed with black and encasing a wine-red flower mass. This is a larger cultivar than some of this type, a mature bush reaching 2 x 2 m and producing hundreds of flowers from autumn

A particularly hardy cultivar, 'Profusion' is very free-flowering.

through winter into spring. Although not long-stemmed enough to be commercially viable as a cut flower, they do last well and are suitable for small arrangements.

This is a notably frost-hardy cultivar, withstanding drops to −5°C without any sign of burning. It will also tolerate moister soils than many proteas, and almost seems to revel in such conditions. A sunny position is desirable to encourage maximum flowering.

H: 2 m	Attracts birds
F: Autumn–spring	Cut flowers
Frost-hardy	

Protea pudens

(previously *P. minor*)

Ground rose, bashful sugarbush

This species is not widely grown by gardeners but is a very suitable subject for rock gardens or spilling over walls and banks. Its sprawling habit (to 40 cm high and 1 m wide), combined with narrow, erectly held foliage and delightful little terminal flowers with brownish-red bracts and a white flower cone tipped with a violet peak, make this an appealing plant that should be more popular with gardeners. Produced during winter to spring in good numbers, the blooms are well displayed but, while they may have some use for small flower arrangements and posies, they are not considered to be commercial.

P. pudens is not regarded as a very hardy species, so

Protea pudens – the bashful ground rose.

sheltered positions will need to be selected in frost-prone gardens. It also requires good air circulation to avoid fungal problems, and therefore should not be crowded. Most well-drained soils, including alkaline ones, suit this species, and it will produce blooms in both sun and semi-shade.

H: 40 cm x 1 m wide	Attracts birds
F: Autumn–winter	Cut flowers (posies)
Medium frost-hardy	

The dainty little *Protea punctata*.

Protea punctata

Water sugarbush

A species that does not attract much attention from gardeners, *P. punctata* nevertheless has a faithful following among floral artists, who appreciate its distinctive and charming little flower heads. Provided these are picked at the soft-bud stage, they will open in a vase and last for a week or so. There are a range of colour variants, ranging from an ivory shade through soft shell-pink to intensely bright pink. The bracts open flat, exposing the central flower mass, which collapses after a few days. These are mainly produced from autumn to midwinter, on a rounded, 2–3 m high bush that may be pruned, keeping within leaf growth, to retain a more compact habit.

This hardy species tolerates both frost and wind well, and is adaptable to a range of free-draining soils.

H: 2–3 m	Frost-hardy
F: Winter–spring	

P. recondita

Hidden sugarbush

P. recondita is rarely offered for sale by nurseries and is something of a collector's item, partly because of its temperamental nature. However, any connoisseur who is able to access this lovely species and has suitable conditions will quickly fall for its charms. Seed is available from time to time from South African sources and is not difficult to germinate.

The blue-frosted glaucous leaves seen in many forms virtually enclose the medium-sized cup-shaped flower heads, though some selections display the blooms more obviously. Red-edged yellowish-green flower bracts surround the large domed flower mass of rusty brown, creating a striking appearance over winter and spring. The low growth habit, to usually little more than 50 cm high but up to 2 m wide with maturity, makes this protea a spectacular subject in a large, sloping rockery or spilling down a bank or retaining wall.

In nature this species grows in rocky mountainous regions of the Cape that experience cold winters and hot dry summers. Similar conditions are required for its successful cultivation. Although *P. recondita* can be grown for a while in humid coastal areas, it will inevitably succumb to disease in these conditions.

H: 50 cm x 2 m wide	Frost-hardy
F: Winter–early spring	

Protea repens

(previously *P. mellifera*)

Sugarbush, common sugarbush

The famed sugarbush, with its copious supplies of sweet nectar so loved by honey-seeking birds, has also been a source of sugar in past years for people living in more isolated areas of South Africa's Cape.

At maturity these large bushes can attain a height of 4 m, but under cultivation it is more usual to see them peaking at 2.5 m, with some pruning and picking helping to keep them within bounds. Narrowly linear, shiny, rich green leaves are a feature of the bush. While usually quite stiff and straight, they may also be long and wavy.

The open funnel-shaped sticky heads of colourful bloom can range from a greenish ice-white through cream to pale pinks and intense reds. Some are larger than others, some are narrow, and others flare wide open in stunning fashion. They are produced at varying times of year according to the origin of the plant:

Protea recondita is not easy to grow but, given the right conditions, is a lovely plant to have in the garden.

ABOVE and RIGHT: *Protea repens*, the common sugarbush, shows many lovely colour variations.

P. revoluta is a delightful collector's item.

P. roupelliae – the long-lived silver sugarbush.

some flower over summer, others during late autumn and winter, and still others over spring. Although the sugarbush is sometimes used as a commercial cut flower, the manner in which the central flower collapses as it develops is seen as a disadvantage in most markets.

The blooms are sought after by birds and bees alike, and it is interesting to invert a cut bloom over a saucer to observe how much nectar drains out over a few hours.

P. repens is a very adaptable species, tolerating a broad range of soils and climatic conditions, and is usually a long-lived and very reliable garden plant that provides a spectacular display.

H: 2– 4.5 m	Attracts birds
F: Depends upon variant	Cut flowers
Medium frost-hardy	

Protea revoluta

Rolled-leaf sugarbush

This little charmer is another species that is usually described as a collector's plant. A suitable subject for a rock garden or retaining wall, it forms a tufted plant just 20 cm high and 1 m across after five or six years, though with age it may reach 2 m wide.

The cup-shaped flower heads, to 60 mm across, are seen over early summer, and their bright lime-green bracts flushed with carmine red are obviously displayed. Foliage is very narrowly linear, up to 250 mm long, and quite distinctive.

P. revoluta naturally grows in an arid, mountainous region of South Africa's Cape, where winters are very cold and summers hot and dry, but it is surprisingly adaptable to a range of conditions provided the climate is not too humid and soils are free-draining. It is both frost-hardy and drought-tolerant once established.

H: 50 cm x 1–2 m wide	Frost-hardy
F: Summer	

Protea roupelliae

Silver sugarbush

This small tree (to 8 m in nature) is more likely to be seen in gardens as a dense shrub of 3 m with an almost equal spread. Its attractive light green foliage sets off brightly coloured red and creamish-green flower heads, which are produced over late summer and autumn when little else is on offer. There is a rarer subspecies, *P. roupelliae* subsp. *hamiltonii*, from the Transvaal that is almost prostrate in growth and has greenish-cream flower heads.

As with most summer-rainfall species of protea, *P. roupelliae* is frost-hardy. It also tolerates snow and is adaptable to a wide range of soil types, including alkaline. A long-lived plant, it eventually becomes rather gnarled with a thick trunk. For the first 20 or so years of its life it is an excellent choice as a screening or background subject in the larger garden.

H: 3 m	Frost-hardy
F: Late summer–autumn	Attracts birds

Protea rubropilosa

Transvaal sugarbush

P. rubropilosa is rarely seen in cultivation but is so outstanding that this summer-rainfall protea should be considered an essential element in the larger protea garden. It is to be hoped that the Transvaal sugarbush becomes more freely available in nurseries.

The large flower heads are comprised of rich red bracts that flare open to reveal the white-tipped, peaked central flower mass. This collapses to become somewhat untidy as it finishes its display but does not detract from the overall appearance. Blooms are produced in large numbers from spring to midsummer.

A large (to 4 m) and very long-lived shrub, it has the advantage of withstanding hard pruning and springing into new growth from old wood. New leaf growth, particularly on selected forms, is a brilliant red, adding further to the appeal of this spectacular species. It is generally frost-hardy and adaptable to a range of soils.

H: 4 m	Frost-hardy
F: Spring–midsummer	Attracts birds

Protea scolymocephala

Small green protea

A very popular species over many years, this protea has become a staple ingredient of floral artists' posy bowls and small table arrangements. Being of a neat habit, it is also valued in smaller gardens.

The cup-shaped 40 mm wide blooms of soft creamy green have a flush of red on the outer bract surfaces, and are produced on fairly short stems over late winter and spring. It is not uncommon to see a mature bush covered with hundreds of flower heads.

Although not often cultivated, *P. rubropilosa* is worthy of a place in the connoisseur's garden.

Protea scolymocephala is a favourite with floral artists.

Generally forming a dense shrub 1 x 1m, it may reach a height of 1.5 m under ideal conditions. Although *P. scolymocephala* thrives in sandy soils in nature, under cultivation some of the best specimens can be seen in quite rich soils derived from river silt. It will withstand some salt wind and is a suitable species for coastal gardens. Frost is tolerated to about –4°C.

H: 1–1.5 m	Medium frost-hardy
F: Late winter–spring	Cut flowers

Protea speciosa

Brown-beard sugarbush

P. speciosa has been cultivated by enthusiasts for many decades, and its distinctive features give it desirability for gardeners and connoisseurs alike.

Growing to little more than 1.2 m high from a strong underground rootstock, which enables it to withstand veld fires and spring into new growth when burned off, this is one of the handful of proteas in cultivation that can be vigorously pruned to ground level. In fact, it is essential to cut back flowering stems to promote bushy growth.

The long flower head, which does not open fully but merely shows a tuft of the cream floral mass within, comprises densely overlapping bracts of ivory or pale pink, which are heavily bearded with dense chocolate-brown fur. These are produced from early spring to mid-summer with a spring peak. Foliage is thick, leathery and, in most cases, quite broad and rounded.

This very long-lived species adapts well to a range of soil types provided they drain freely, and it will surive frost to –4°C. Watering is necessary in dry summers.

H: 1.2 m	Attracts birds
F: Mainly spring	Cut flowers
Medium frost-hardy	

Protea stokoei

Stokoe's protea, pink sugarbush

A handsome, erect-growing shrub, 2–3 m tall at maturity, *P. stokoei* has very distinctive flower heads and leaves. Unfortunately, because it is difficult to propagate, it is not often offered by the nursery trade.

The deep grey-green leaves are borne densely and are broadly oval in shape, leathery, red-margined and, when young, are fringed with silky hair. Flower heads are a soft pink shade, with the tip of each bract densely tipped

The unusual *Protea speciosa* has long been a favourite garden plant.

with rich brown fur. This is most apparent at the apex of the flower head, where they curve inwards, the cream inner flower just showing as a tuft. The main flowering period is winter and spring. Although not often seen as a cut flower, both the heads and foliage of the pink sugarbush have excellent lasting qualities.

This is regarded as a difficult subject under cultivation in its native South Africa, but in some countries, notably New Zealand, in the right conditions of temperate climate with moist but free-draining acidic soils, old specimens bloom prolifically.

H: 2–3 m	Attracts birds
F: Winter–spring	Cut flowers
Tolerates light frosts	

Protea sulphurea

Sulphur-coloured protea, sulphur sugarbush

One of the loveliest protea species for both groundcover and spilling over walls and down banks, *P. sulphurea* offers a startling contrast between its large lantern-like blooms and the small neat foliage. The flowers may be up to 130 mm wide at their peak development, and are carried like glowing lanterns from autumn through winter. The reverse of the overlapping bracts is a greenish shade edged with red, while the inner surfaces and the base of the floral mass is a beautiful sulphur-yellow and is sometimes likened to a stained-glass window. The peak of the flower mass is a deep golden bronze. In nature a variant is known with red bracts.

The very distinctive small (30 mm long and 10 mm wide) glaucous green leaves clothe the sprawling or mounding bush, which can either mound up into a cushion of 50–70 cm high and several metres wide or cascade down banks and walls in a dense mat to a distance of 3 m or so. It is easily kept trimmed to a more manageable size in the home garden.

This frost-hardy species prefers sunny positions in order to flower well, and it appreciates well-drained, lighter soils that are not high in nutrients.

H: 50–70 cm x 2–3 m wide	Limited cut-flower
F: Winter–spring	potential
Frost-hardy	

RIGHT TOP: The pink sugarbush, *Protea stokoei*, is a highly distinctive and beautiful species.

RIGHT: *P. sulphurea* is one of the loveliest hanging proteas.

Protea 'Thomas'

An Australian introduction from South African Harry Woods, who now lives in Western Australia, 'Thomas' is a lovely hybrid of *P. compacta* parentage that shows similarities to the New Zealand 'Franciscan Hybrid'. It highlights the valuable characteristics of neat, medium-sized flower heads, clear colour and long stems, combined with vigour that this parentage imparts to the resulting progeny. *P. magnifica* is frequently being used as one of the other parents in this cross.

'Thomas' forms a neat, bushy cultivar to 2 m that produces its prominently displayed rich pink blooms during winter to spring. The bracts shade to cream at the base and the central floral mass is distinctively peaked. It is both a striking garden plant and a good cut-flower subject.

As is typical of this type of cultivar, 'Thomas' is frost-hardy to –4°C once established, requires well-drained soil and a sunny position, and is reasonably wind-tolerant.

LEFT: 'Thomas' – an interesting Australian introduction.

BELOW and RIGHT: The beautiful new *Protea* 'Venus'.

H: 2 m	Attracts birds
F: Winter–spring	Cut flowers
Medium frost-hardy	

Protea 'Venus'

This very handsome cultivar, which was developed in South Africa, could well become one of the most sought-after and spectacular new horticultural releases of the first decade of the twenty-first century. A *P. aristata* x *P. repens* cross, the first commercial hybrid of this parentage to be released, this protea should prove to be an outstandingly successful cut flower and garden plant.

The foliage is intermediate between the parent plants, being linear, glaucous and of medium length, to 100–120 mm. The large blooms are carried on long, sturdy, straight stems and are to be seen over spring and early summer. Commencing as a deep reddish-brown bud with the overlapping bracts edged with silvery-white hair, this opens to a flower head that looks like a large, deeper red version of *P. aristata*.

The bush is vigorous, of erect growth to 2–2.5 m,

and produces its blooms freely from an early age. Given its parentage, 'Venus' should prove adaptable to a wide range of free-draining soils, be quite frost-hardy and generally easy to grow for most gardeners.

H: 2–2.5 m	Attracts birds
F: Spring–summer	Cut flowers
Frost-hardy	

Protea venusta

Creeping beauty

This low-growing protea develops into a mounding or broadly spreading bush of some 2–3 m wide but just 70 cm to 1 m high. Its horizontal or slightly pendulous branches bear small flower heads that open from bright pink in bud to an attractive combination of pink and white, with the flower mass forming a tight 'shuttlecock' of white. Flowering time is over late summer, when few other protea species perform, which adds to its value in the garden. There are several slightly larger variants that are less attractive than the one described here.

P. venusta is a very suitable choice for covering a bank or arching over a wall. It can also look very effective in a larger rock garden with its flowering branches trailing between large boulders.

Noted for withstanding frosts and even light snowfalls, this species is adaptable to most well-drained soils in both sunny and partially shaded positions. It is wind-tolerant and very suitable for cold inland districts where other protea species may not survive. It does not thrive in humid environments, where it will prove shy to flower and subject to fungal disease.

H: 70 cm–1 m x 2–3 m wide	Frost-hardy
F: Late summer	

P. venusta is a frost-hardy montane species.

SERRURIA

This delightful genus of 44 species from South Africa's south-western Cape has achieved something of a connoisseur status among gardeners, partly because of its relative rarity in cultivation and because of its fairly tender nature and specific cultural requirements.

The beautiful *Serruria florida,* the blushing bride, which is rare in nature, a superb cut flower and sought after for floristry, is the best-known member of the genus. In recent times it has become more readily available to gardeners and cut-flower growers, and has been used with excellent results in hybridising work with *S. rosea* ('Sugar 'n' Spice' and 'Carmen').

Particularly in Australia, the compact new *Serruria* cultivars have become popular container plants. Potting mixes for these must be very free-draining and low in nutrients. Plants should be pruned back immediately after flowering to ensure compact growth habits.

Serruria aemula

Strawberry spiderhead

This delightful little curiosity so well suited to rock gardens and tub culture appears only occasionally in nurseries and is usually snapped up when it does.

While *Serruria aemula* may be small-flowered, this does not prevent the show provided through sheer volume of flower when it throws its display during late winter and spring. Commencing as little tuft-like heads of bright pink, the flowers lighten to a pale pink as they develop, thus creating a multi-coloured appearance. At times they almost appear intertwined with the fine, net-like foliage, which deepens to a reddish colouring in colder weather. Although of no real use for picking, this little bush, which reaches no more than 50 cm in height at most, is at its best in tubs, in the foreground of shrub borders or in rockeries.

RIGHT: The free-flowering *Serruria* 'Carmen' is an excellent subject for cultivating in a tub.

Well-drained, lighter soils are essential for this and other *Serruria* species, and only light frosts are tolerated. They prefer full sun if they are to flower well, are fertiliser-sensitive and need to be lightly pruned after flowering to encourage new growth and a compact, bushy growth habit.

H: 50 cm	Tolerates light frosts
F: Winter–spring	

The dainty little *S. aemula* is an ideal species for the tub or planter.

Serruria 'Carmen'

This beautiful cultivar, developed by the ARC Fynbos Unit in South Africa, is of the same *S. florida* x *S. rosea* parentage as the earlier-developed 'Sugar 'n' Spice' and has been heavily promoted in Australia. It can be grown as either a shrub in borders or planters, or as a highly successful tub plant provided suitable potting mixes are used (see below).

Growing to a bushy shrub of 1 x 1 m in the garden or in larger tubs, 'Carmen' differs from its sibling in being of a more compact habit and having fuller, more rounded bracts. Initially pale, these develop into an intense pinkish red. It is extremely free-flowering, a mature bush producing hundreds of little clustered flower heads. While not as popular for cut-flower purposes as *S. florida*, these can be used to wonderful effect in posies and similar smaller arrangements. The main flowering period is considerably later than 'Sugar 'n' Spice', from late winter through spring.

All *Serruria* species and cultivars require well-drained soils and are sensitive to fertilisers, especially those with high phosphate levels. In tubs it is important to use potting mixes formulated for proteaceous plants or to obtain mixes without fertiliser to which small amounts of low-phosphate slow-release fertiliser can be added ('Osmocote for Australian Natives' is ideal). Tubbed plants should be watered daily except during wet weather. They should be lightly pruned (keeping well within the leaf growth area of the stems) after flowering, in early summer. As tubbed plants outgrow their containers they should be gradually moved up into slightly larger tubs; they should not be 'overpotted'. Serrurias are frost-sensitive, with temperatures below –1 or –2°C likely to damage, and prefer sunny positions to encourage both flowering and robust growth.

Photograph on page 167

H: 1 m	Tolerates light frosts
F: Winter–spring	Cut flowers

Serruria florida

Blushing bride

The most sought-after of serrurias, and indeed one of the most famed members of the South African Proteaceae, *S. florida* was 'lost' for some 90 years, believed by botanists to have become extinct, and was rediscovered in 1891. It received its common name through the custom of young men in South Africa's Cape wearing the flowers in buttonholes when courting.

The spectacular heads of bloom produced during winter and spring are 5 cm long and have white bracts, softly flushed pink, surrounding the tight central floral mass of pink. These are borne in clusters of up to eight and carried on long stems, making them very popular with florists, particularly in view of their prolonged vase life. They also dry easily to extend their useful life for an almost indefinite period.

Delicately divided, long and narrow, almost needle-shaped leaflets give an overall feathery appearance to *S. florida*. If the bush is not pruned or picked, it will quickly become 'leggy' or spindly, so it is essential to prune bushes well back (keeping within leaf growth) as flowering finishes. This should result in a bushy, dense shrub of 1–1.5 m and will also provide many more blooms. No more than a degree or two of frost is normally tolerated by this splendid species, which it is at its best in temperate climates, in well-drained soils and sunny positions.

| H: 1–1.5 m | Tolerates light frosts |
| F: Winter–spring | Cut flowers |

An unusually large specimen of *S. florida*.

Serruria florida – the beautiful blushing bride.

Serruria glomerata

Cluster spiderhead

An unusual plant, *S. glomerata* is occasionally offered by nurseries, and the illustration depicts a selected form being marketed as 'Lemon Honey', which seems to have a more compact habit than the usual species.

This is a very suitable specimen for tub culture that will retain a neat habit and bloom freely if it is lightly pruned as flowering finishes. The distinctive clustered round heads of bloom are a delightful cream shade, which contrasts strikingly with the dense, much-divided, fine foliage. Produced over much of spring, these flowers are especially ornamental when the plant is used in a container, such as a terracotta pot, that introduces a third colour.

Serruria glomerata ranges from 30 to 70 cm in height and has the same requirements as *S.* 'Carmen'.

| H: 30–70 cm | Tolerates light frosts |
| F: Spring | Cut flowers |

Serruria glomerata makes a charming tub plant.

Serruria pedunculata

(previously *S. artemesiaefolia*)

Grey serruria, fan-leaf spiderhead

The grey serruria, though never widely available, has been cultivated by keen gardeners in South Africa and New Zealand for many decades. Its blooms are not spectacular in the usual sense, but their unusual colouring and the overall effect of this small shrub combine to produce an intriguing shrub.

S. *pedunculata*'s growth habit is low (50 cm to 1 m) and spreading. Foliage is delicately divided, fan-shaped and a grey-green colour, which gives the plant a 'cloudy' or 'smoky' appearance. This impression is enhanced by the blooms, which open from silky-grey buds to flower heads of purplish-wine to pink tonings. This display takes place from late winter through spring into the early months of summer.

While not normally recognised as a being a cut-flower

The grey serruria has novelty value.

subject, the blooms are sometimes used effectively in smaller arrangements, where they last well.

Cultural requirements are as for S. 'Carmen'.

| H: 50 cm – 1 m | Tolerates light frosts |
| F: Spring | Cut flowers |

Serruria phylicoides

(previously *S. barbigera*)

Silky serruria, bearded spiderhead.

One of the many smaller-flowered *Serruria* species, S. *phylicoides* is another that is extremely free-flowering, becoming almost smothered from late winter to early summer with silken heads tipped with silver. As these open and reflex, they become a deep red, giving an overall silvery-pink appearance. A deep red 'Highland Form' is rare in cultivation. There is potential for floral use of both in posies and for infill in arrangements.

This species develops into a bushy shrub of some 60 cm high. The finely divided feathery foliage is generally a deep green colour but often assumes a reddish cast, especially during winter or in poor soils. The silky serruria is an attractive choice for tubs, planters or small borders. Light pruning after flowering is essential to maintain a neat growth habit.

Typically, this *Serruria* requires free-draining soils or potting mixes, protection from all but the lightest frost, a sunny position and general avoidance of fertilisers.

| H: 60 cm | Tolerates light frosts |
| F: Spring | Cut flowers |

S. phylicoides produces a massed display in spring.

Serruria 'Sugar 'n' Spice'

A very popular tub plant in Australia – where it was developed by Proteaflora Nursery – this *S. florida* x *S. rosea* cultivar has been well received by gardeners in other countries, including New Zealand, where it is also used in the foreground of shrub borders and rockeries.

A compact, very free-flowering and colourful small plant, 'Sugar 'n' Spice' can, with a little care, make a spectacular tubbed specimen. It fact it is probably better suited to this usage than for growing in the open ground. (See *Serruria* 'Carmen' for tips for growing in containers.) Under these conditions it will gradually become a shapely bush of 1 m high with a nearly equal spread and can produce hundreds of flower heads from midwinter to spring. These are occasionally used by florists for appealing posies and buttonholes.

Cultural requirements are as for *S.* 'Carmen'.

A massed display of flowers is a feature of 'Sugar 'n' Spice'.
INSET: *Serruria rosea* is one of the parents of this hybrid.

The lovely *Serruria* 'Sugar 'n' Spice' is an excellent tub plant.

| H: 1 m | Tolerates light frosts |
| F: Winter–spring | Cut flowers |

STENOCARPUS

ABOVE: *Stenocarpus sinuatus*, the Queensland firewheel tree, is well named for its brilliant displays during autumn and winter.

BELOW: The bud stage shows the 'wheel' and its 'spokes' to best advantage.

There are at least 27 species of *Stenocarpus*, with most being native to New Caledonia. Eight are found in Australia and two in Papua New Guinea. They are either tall shrubs or trees, and the most widely grown under cultivation is undoubtedly *S. sinuatus*. While others have handsome foliage and appealing growth habits, this is the only one to have spectacular flowers.

Stenocarpus sinuatus

Queensland firewheel tree, wheel of fire, white silky oak

The appropriately named Queensland firewheel tree is handsome whether in flower or not, with its large, glossy green leaves of extremely variable form adding to its considerable appeal. Native to northern New South Wales, extending into Queensland, and also Papua New Guinea, it is widely grown in many parts of Australia, New Zealand, warmer parts of the United States and other countries as a specimen and street tree, its neat dimensions making it very suitable for these purposes.

  S. sinuatus is normally an upright, non-spreading tree

of up to 35 m in its natural rainforest environment, but under cultivation it rarely exceeds a height of 14 m. The glossy leaves may be entire (without teeth or divisions) but still with wavy margins, while others may be only slightly divided, or deeply and irregularly lobed and divided; all this occurring on the same tree. The flowers, such a feature of this species, are arranged like the spokes of a wheel. These 'wheels' in turn may be carried in thick clusters on the branches, with each individual flower, or 'spoke' of the wheel, being a bright scarlet with the globular apex a rich gold. The overall effect is like a tree laden with firewheels, producing a startling display over autumn into winter.

This is a surprisingly easy tree to grow, being adaptable to both light and heavy soils provided they are fertile and free-draining yet receiving adequate moisture. It will thrive in sun or semi-shade and is hardy to at least –4°C once well established. Because of its neat shape, it can be grown in quite small gardens and in its early years can be used as a handsome tub plant.

H: 14–35 m	Frost-hardy
F: Autumn–winter	

TELOPEA

Telopeas, or waratahs as they are better known, are among the most spectacular Australian members of the Proteaceae. There are just four species, with habitats ranging from New South Wales and Victoria to Tasmania. Within these species there are marked variations in colour and shape of the spectacular flower heads.

The New South Wales waratah, *T. speciosissima*, is the most variable species and is a superb long-lasting cut flower. It has become a significant crop for both local and export markets in several other countries.

The Victorian waratah, *T. oreades*, is also known as the Gippsland waratah, while the other two species – the Tasmanian waratah, *T. truncata* (which also has a yellow variant), and the Braidwood or Monga waratah, *T. mongaensis*, are not described here because, by comparison, they have little horticultural merit.

Waratahs have an undeserved reputation of being temperamental and difficult to establish under cultivation. The basic requirements are fairly good, well-drained, acidic soil in a reasonably sunny position. Some shelter from strong winds is desirable, and it is imperative to prune back as flowering finishes.

Telopea 'Burgundy'

A particularly hardy and prolific cultivar, 'Burgundy' has the added attributes of being easier to grow than *T. speciosissima*. It is also earlier flowering, sometimes producing the odd bloom out of season, during autumn. This is a *T. speciosissima* x *T. oreades* cultivar that has been marketed under other names, and there have been a number of similar cultivars selected, particularly in Australia. Many of these are naturally occurring hybrids where species overlap in the natural habitat or even under cultivation.

As with so many hybrids, 'Burgundy' is vigorous, rapidly growing to a dense shrub of 3–4 m in height, and with the heavy pruning so necessary after flowering, it quickly becomes densely multi-trunked. It has the smooth-edged foliage of the *T. oreades* parent, and the domed flower heads of deep crimson are midway between the parents, having the colouring of *T. oreades*

'Burgundy' is a vigorous and hardy *Telopea* cultivar.

173

but more of the *T. speciosissima* shape. Blooms are produced on very long stems, often a metre or more, in large numbers during late winter and early spring, with odd flowers in autumn. While not as successful for cut-flower purposes as *T. speciosissima*, it is widely used for this purpose by growers in some districts.

The main requirements for successful cultivation are reasonably fertile, acidic soils that have a good humus content, retain moisture and yet drain freely. Some shelter from wind is desirable, and this cultivar will perform well in both sun or partial shade. It is frost-hardy to at least –8°C.

H: 3–4 m	Attracts birds
F: Winter–spring	Cut flowers
Frost-hardy	

Telopea oreades

Victorian waratah, tree waratah, Gippsland waratah

T. oreades, the Victorian waratah, is notable for being the hardiest species and particularly long-lived. It is sometimes used in hybridising and as a rootstock for grafting selections of *T. speciosissima* that have proved difficult to strike from cuttings, although tissue culture is now bypassing this technique. While it is not often used as a garden plant today, with the abundance of spectacular cultivars on offer, *T. oreades* does still have a place in gardens prone to very hard frosts, and it also can make an ornamental background plant when left to assume its natural habit as a 12 m high, broadly branched tree. Kept pruned and shaped, it will form a larger and spectacular specimen shrub.

Telopea oreades, the Victorian waratah, is very frost-hardy.

The flower heads of deep crimson colouring are distinguished from the better-known *T. speciosissima* by their flat-topped and open shape. They are produced during spring, and in higher altitudes or colder districts may appear up to a month later than in mild climates. Leaf margins are smooth, lacking the teeth or serrations of the New South Wales waratah.

This species has been recorded as surviving happily in gardens subject to frosts as low as –15°C. It prefers reasonably fertile, well-drained soils that retain some moisture over summer.

H: To 12 m	Frost-hardy
F: Spring	Attracts birds

Telopea speciosissima

New South Wales waratah

A spectacular multi-stemmed erect shrub up to 4 m high, this best known of the waratahs (and the state floral emblem of New South Wales) usually produces large, rich red flower heads on long, stout stems. These are dramatically displayed during spring, with mature well-pruned bushes providing up to 400 blooms in a season. This is a significantly variable species with many named cultivars. These range in colour from a naturally occurring white variant ('Wirrimbirra White') through varying shades of red, sometimes tipped with silver, Flower heads may differ in both size and shape, some being quite squat, others decidedly dome-shaped. The basal bracts, too, vary in size. Manipulated hybrids with both *T. oreades* and the Tasmanian waratah, *T. truncata*, are also promoted by nurseries.

This is one of the more frost-hardy members of the *Proteaceae*, being able to withstand occasional winter temperatures as low as –7°C. It is particularly important to prune immediately after flowering to maintain a compact habit. Very old 'leggy' plants are sometimes pruned using a chainsaw. Reasonably good, well-drained soils and some protection from wind are also desirable for successful cultivation.

A spectacular garden shrub, *T. speciosissima* has also become a successful commercial flower crop, notably in Australia, New Zealand, Hawaii and Zimbabwe. Large quantities are shipped to eager markets in Japan and the United States.

H: 3–4 m	Attracts birds
F: Winter–spring	Cut flowers
Frost-hardy	

ABOVE: A particularly lovely, selected form of the spectacular New South Wales waratah.

LEFT: Another form of *Telopea speciosissima*, with silvery-white tips to the individual buds.

BELOW: 'Wirrimbirra White' – the white waratah – has become readily available to gardeners in recent years.

The New Zealand toru is a very ornamental shrub or small tree with a neat habit, glossy foliage and scented flowers.

TORONIA

This genus with a single species, *Toronia toru*, was formerly classified as part of the *Persoonia* genus. It is one of the two New Zealand members of the Proteaceae.

Toronia toru

(previously *Persoonia toru*)

Toru

T. toru is a delightful large shrub or small (to 7 m) tree of neat, symmetrical proportions that make it well suited to many garden situations.

The elegant narrow leaves are shiny, quite thick and mid-green, sometimes with red tones. Young growth is an attractive rusty orange-brown colour.

The small cream to orange-brown flowers are produced en masse over late spring and summer and are carried on red, hairy stems that spring from the leaf axils. The blooms are very sweetly scented – on warm evenings their perfume can permeate a garden – and are followed by small red nut-like fruit.

The toru, as it is commonly known in New Zealand, is best grown in either full sun or partial shade and should ideally be given space to show off its symmetry. It is frost-hardy to about –6°C once established and can be grown in a wide range of soils. In dry positions some summer watering is advantageous.

H: To 7 m	Medium frost-hardy
F: Summer	

Glossary

acid: in reference to soil; with a pH value of less than 7.0. The lower the figure, the higher the acidity: e.g. pH3 is strongly acidic.

aeration: used in reference to soils comprising larger particles that allow air spaces between them. Soils with poor aeration are usually made up of fine particles with little air space and have a tendency to become waterlogged.

alba: from the Latin *albus*, meaning white. Used to denote white-flowered variants,

alkaline: in reference to the soil; with a pH value of more than 7.0. The higher the figure, the greater the alkalinity: e.g. pH11 is strongly alkaline.

apex: the tip of an organ, such as a leaf.

aurea: from the Latin *aurum*, meaning golden. Used to denote yellow- or gold-flowered variants.

awn: a fine, bearded or bristle-like appendage.

bract: a modified leaf. Usually surrounding a flower. Particularly used in reference to leucadendrons.

bypass: term used to describe new shoots arising from the stem just below a flower and extending beyond the bloom while it is still opening. May be regarded as an undesirable feature for commercial picking purposes.

chlorosis: yellowing of foliage, usually because of a nutrient deficiency, but may also be due to a toxic condition.

clone: a group of individuals produced by asexual reproduction and therefore exactly alike.

corymb: a flat-topped or convex and open flower cluster. A raceme in which the stalks of the lower flowers are longer than those of the flowers above, bringing all flowers to a similar level.

cultivar: from *culti* vated *vari*ety. One that has arisen, been cultivated, propagated, proved to be reliably persistent and named to comply with internationally accepted rules.

cultivation: term used to describe conditions under which plants grow successfully in the home garden.

dioecious: having male and female flowers on separate plants.

entire: used in reference to leaves; with an even margin, without toothing or divisions.

erect: of upright habit.

floriferous: term used to describe a very free-flowering habit.

forms: term used loosely to cover different variants of a species.

fungicide: chemical used to control fungous diseases.

genera: plural of genus.

genus: smallest natural group that contains related species and is intermediate between the family and species.

glabrous: smooth, without hairs.

glaucous: blue-green in colouring and/or covered with a powdery bloom.

habit: the overall appearance and growth form of a plant.

habitat: natural home of a plant or animal.

humus: organic matter in an advanced state of decomposition.

hybrid: progeny resulting from the crossing between two species.

inflorescence: a cluster of flowers or a flower head.

involucral: a ring of bracts or leaves surrounding flowers.

lanceolate: lance-shaped, narrow, tapering at both ends. Used in describing leaf shape.

lateral: occurring at the side of an organ.

lignotuber: swollen axis of a plant at the base of the stem possessing dormant buds capable of sprouting.

lignotuberous: persistent rootstock as in *Telopea*

speciosissima, Banksia robur, Protea cynaroides and various other members of the Proteaceae.

luteum: from the Latin *luteus*, meaning yellow.

margin: the edge of a leaf.

mulch: loose material laid down to protect roots of plants. Also used to describe other soil coverings such as the various plastic types available.

neutral: used to denote pH7. Neither acid nor alkaline.

oxidising: combining with oxygen, used in reference to blackening of protea leaves after harvesting of blooms.

pathogen: organism or substance causing disease.

pendent: hanging.

pendulous: of hanging habit: e.g., flower heads of *Protea nana.*

perianth: the floral parts outside the stamens; calyx and corolla of the flowers.

pH: a measure of acidity or alkalinity of a substance. pH 7 is neutral; above that figure is alkaline, below it is acid.

proteoid: term applied to fine rootlets of proteaceous plants.

pubescent: covered with short, soft or silky hairs.

reflex: bend or turn sharply backwards.

rootstock: a rhizome.

scale: 1. Term used to describe lower bracts on protea flowerheads. 2. Scale insects; hard, white, brown or black flattened insects that fasten on to leaves and stems.

semi-hardwood: growth that has begun to firm up, usually between spring and winter. Term applied to cutting material that is at the correct stage for propagating from, often in autumn.

species: singular or plural term to denote units within a genus that are distinguishable from each other.

sport: a variation from the normal type.

stamen: pollen-producing part of a flower, comprising anther and filament.

style: slender part of the pistil in a flower, carrying the pollen-receiving stigma.

subspecies: between a species and a variety.

systemic: term used, in the case of spray chemicals, to indicate those that are absorbed or translocated through the plant sap stream, either through the roots or the foliage.

terminal: in flower heads, relating to those borne at the tip or apex of the stem.

tomentum: dense, short hairs often located on the undersides of foliage or on stems of young growth.

toxicity: term used for condition caused through excessive uptake of elements: e.g. phosphorous toxicity in the case of proteaceous plants.

variant: form arising from a variation. A definable individual plant or group of, displaying differences from the normal species.

variety: plant that is subordinate to a species or subspecies and has been validly and legitimately named and published in accordance with the rules of nomenclature.

veld: (from the Dutch *veld*, formerly *veldt*) open, unforested or lightly forested grass-country in South Africa.

xylem: woody tissue within the stem of a plant, comprising vessels and fibres concerned with transportation of solutions from the roots.

References and recommended reading

Blombery, Alec & Mahoney, Betty. *Proteaceae of the Sydney Region*, Angus & Robertson, Sydney, 1981.

Burke, Don. 1983. *Growing Grevilleas*, Kangaroo Press, Sydney, 1983.

Eliovsen, Sima. 1973. *Proteas for Pleasure*, MacMillan, Johannesburg, 1973.

George, Alex S. *The Genus Banksia*. Nuytsia, vol. 3. Western Australia, 1981.

George, Alex S. *The Banksia Book*, Kangaroo Press, Sydney, 1984.

George, Alex S. *An Introduction to the Proteaceae of Western Australia*, Kangaroo Press, Sydney, 1984

Hocking, P. J. & M. B. Thomas. 'Evolution of the Proteaceae and Cultural Implications', *Royal New Zealand Institute of Horticulture Annual*, 1974.

Holliday, Ivan & Geoffrey Watton. *A Field Guide to Banksias*, Rigby, Sydney, 1975.

Kepler, Angela Kay. *Proteas in Hawaii*, Mutual, Honolulu, Hawaii, 1988.

McGillivray, D. J. *Grevillea (Proteaceae)*, Melbourne University Press, 1993.

McLennan, Rob. *Growing Proteas*, Kangaroo Press, Sydney, 1993.

Matthews. Lewis J. *South African Proteaceae in New Zealand*, Matthews, N.Z., 1983.

Matthews, Lewis J. *The Protea Growers Handbook*, Bateman, Auckland, 1983.

Matthews, Lewis J. *Proteas of the World*, Bateman, Auckland, 1993.

Nixon, Paul. *The Waratah*, Kangaroo Press, Sydney, 1987.

Rebelo, Tony. *Sasol Proteas: A Field Guide to the Proteas of Southern Africa*, Fernwood Press, Vlaeberg, 1995.

Rousseau, Frank. *The Proteaceae of South Africa*, Purnell, Cape Town, 1970.

Rourke, John P. 'Taxonomic Studies on Leucospermum', *Journal of South African Botany*, vol. 8, 1972.

Rourke, John P. *The Proteas of Southern Africa*, Purnell, Cape Town, 1980.

Vogts, Marie M. *South Africa's Proteaceae; Know Them and Grow Them*, Struik, Cape Town, 1982.

Williams, Ion J. M. *A Revision of the Genus Leucadendron (Proteaceae)*, Contributions from the Bolus Herbarium, no. 3, Cape Town, 1972.

Wrigley, John W. & Murray Fagg. *Banksias, Waratahs and All Other Plants in the Australian Proteaceae Family*, Collins, Sydney, 1989.

Index